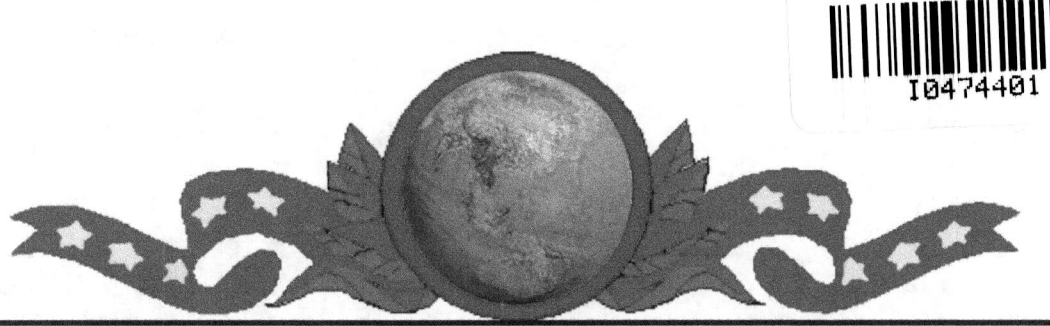

# Real World
## Colouring Book
### For Advanced Users & Adults

Copyright 2019 By John Boom

## 50 Images

## Created From Real Life Photos
## For You To Colour As You Please.

ISBN 978-0-359-93590-1
90000

9 780359 935901

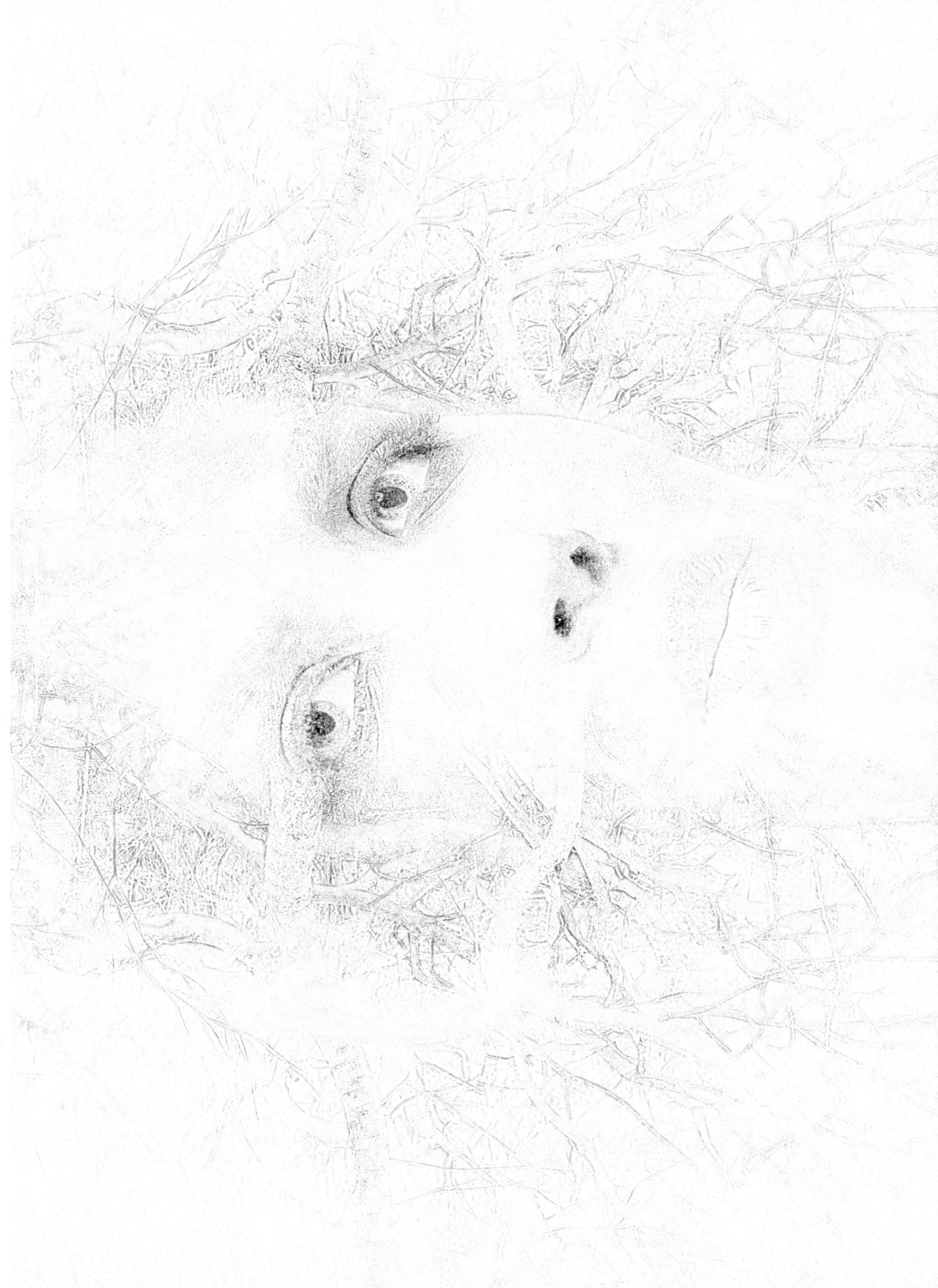

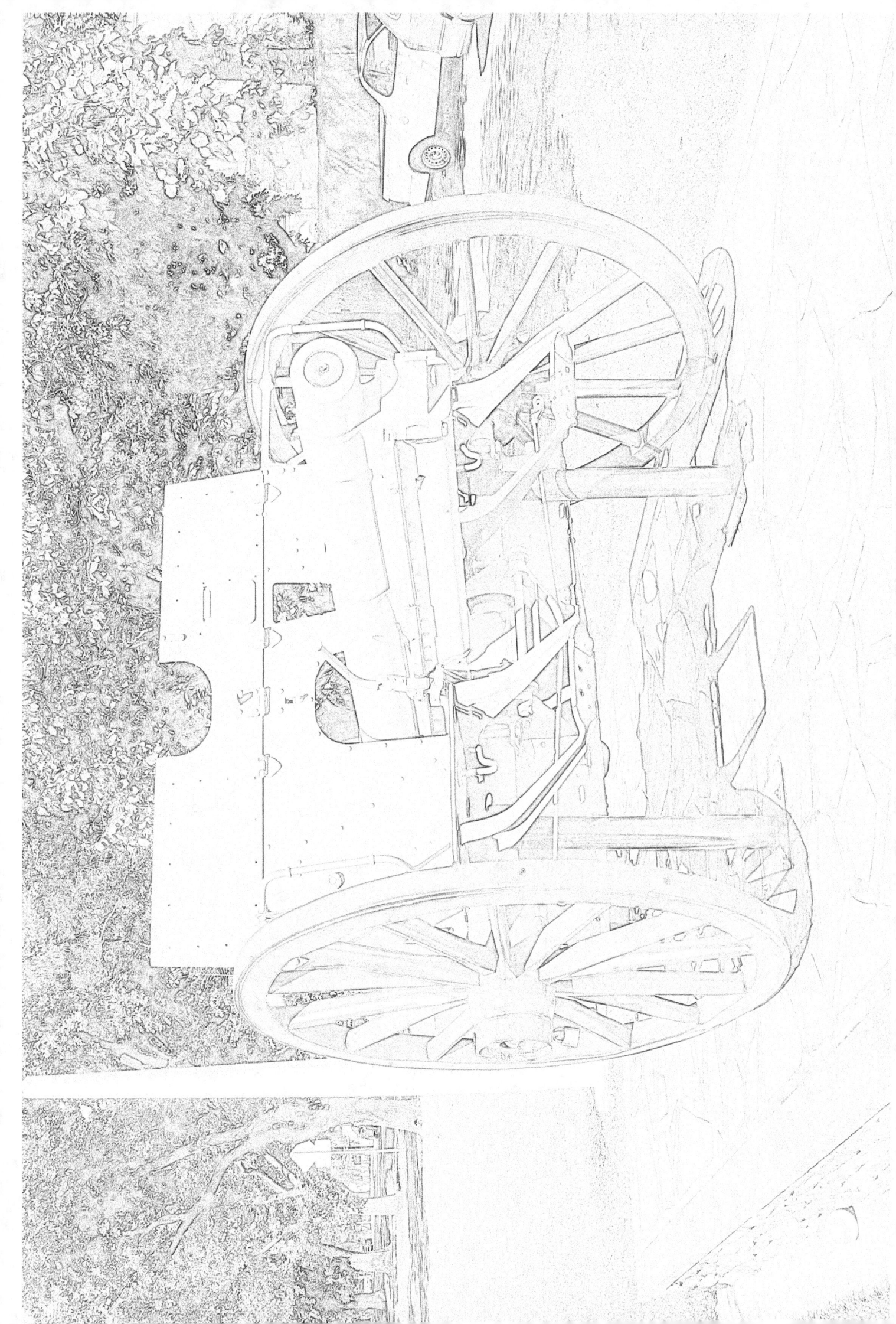

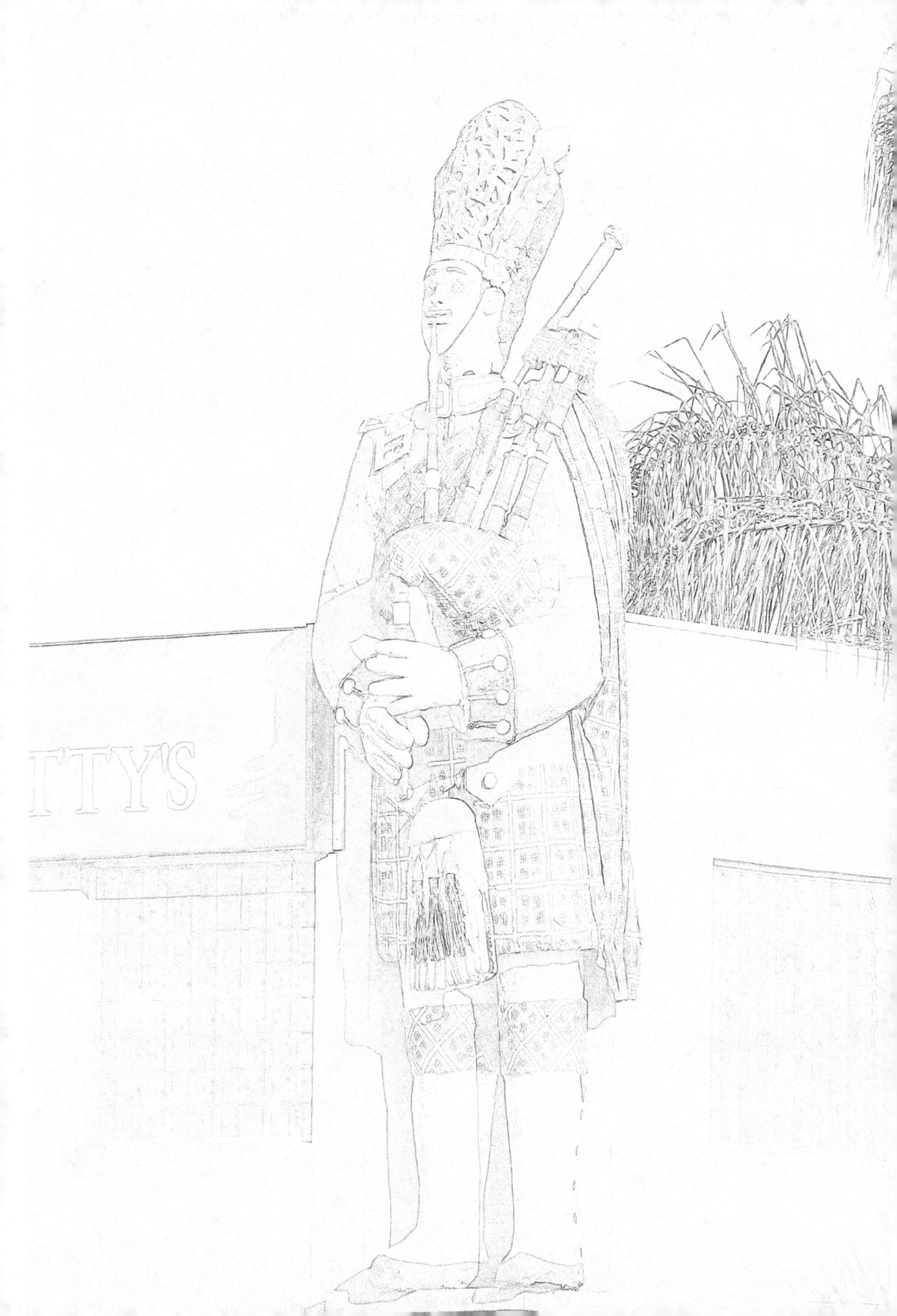

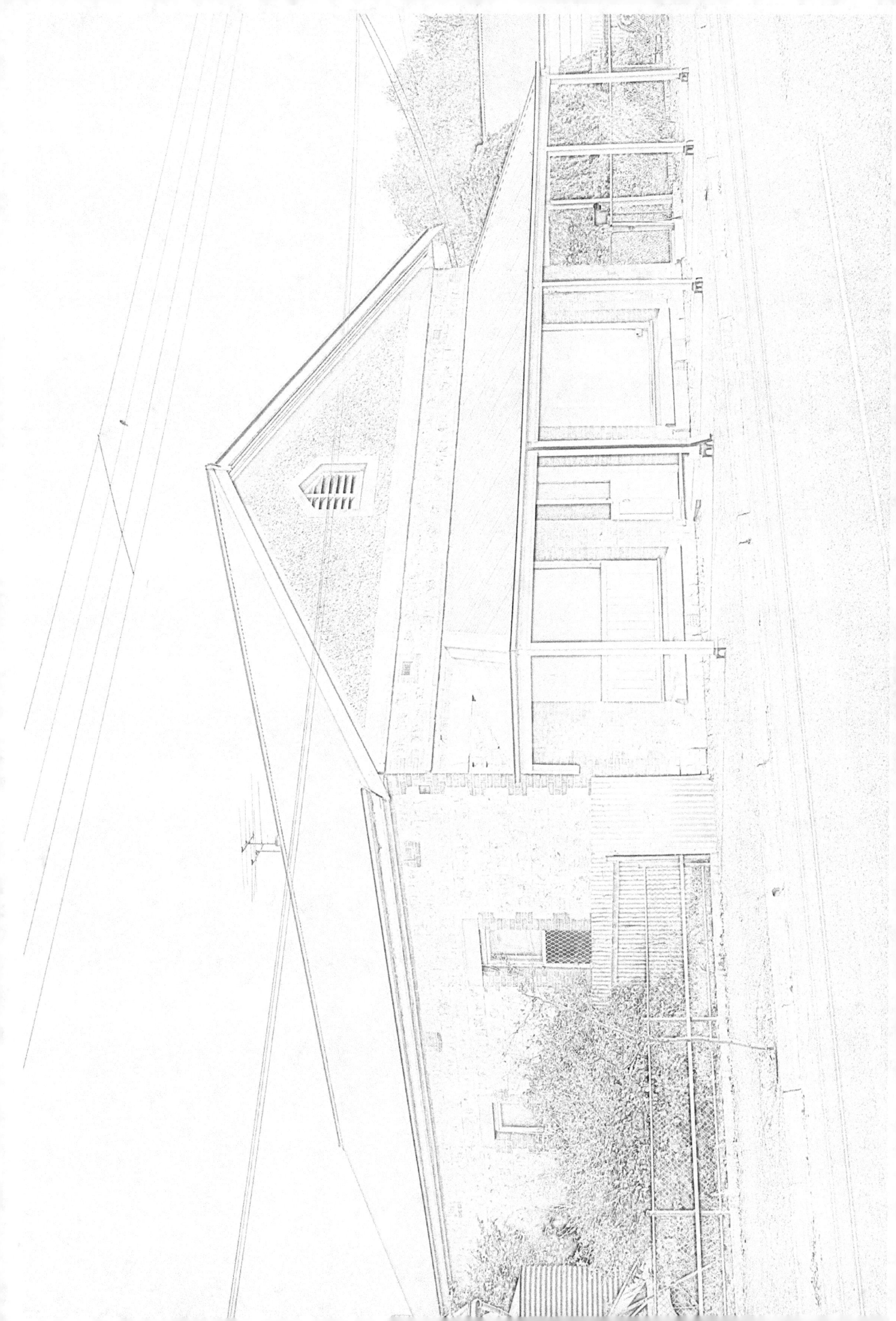

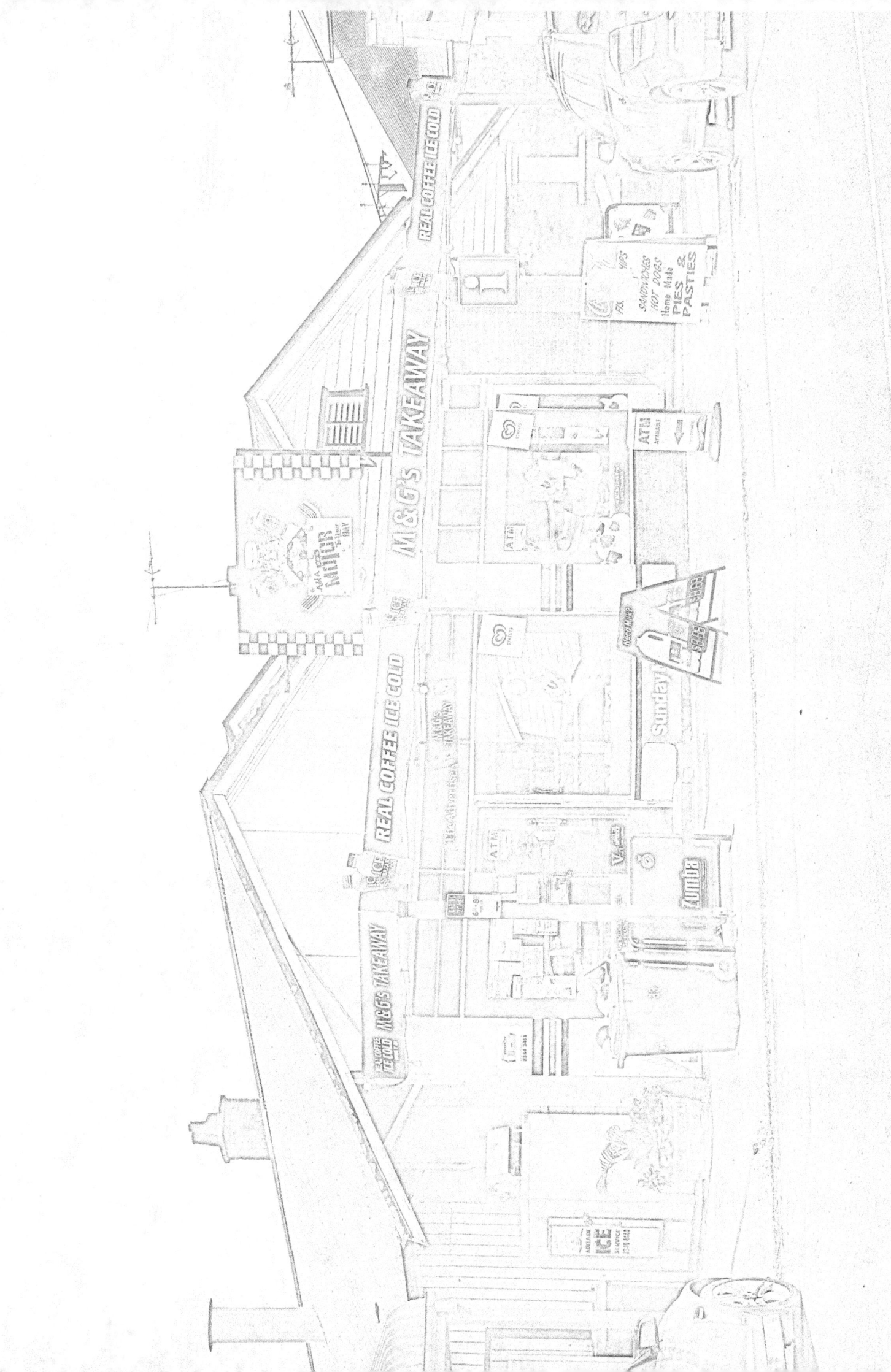

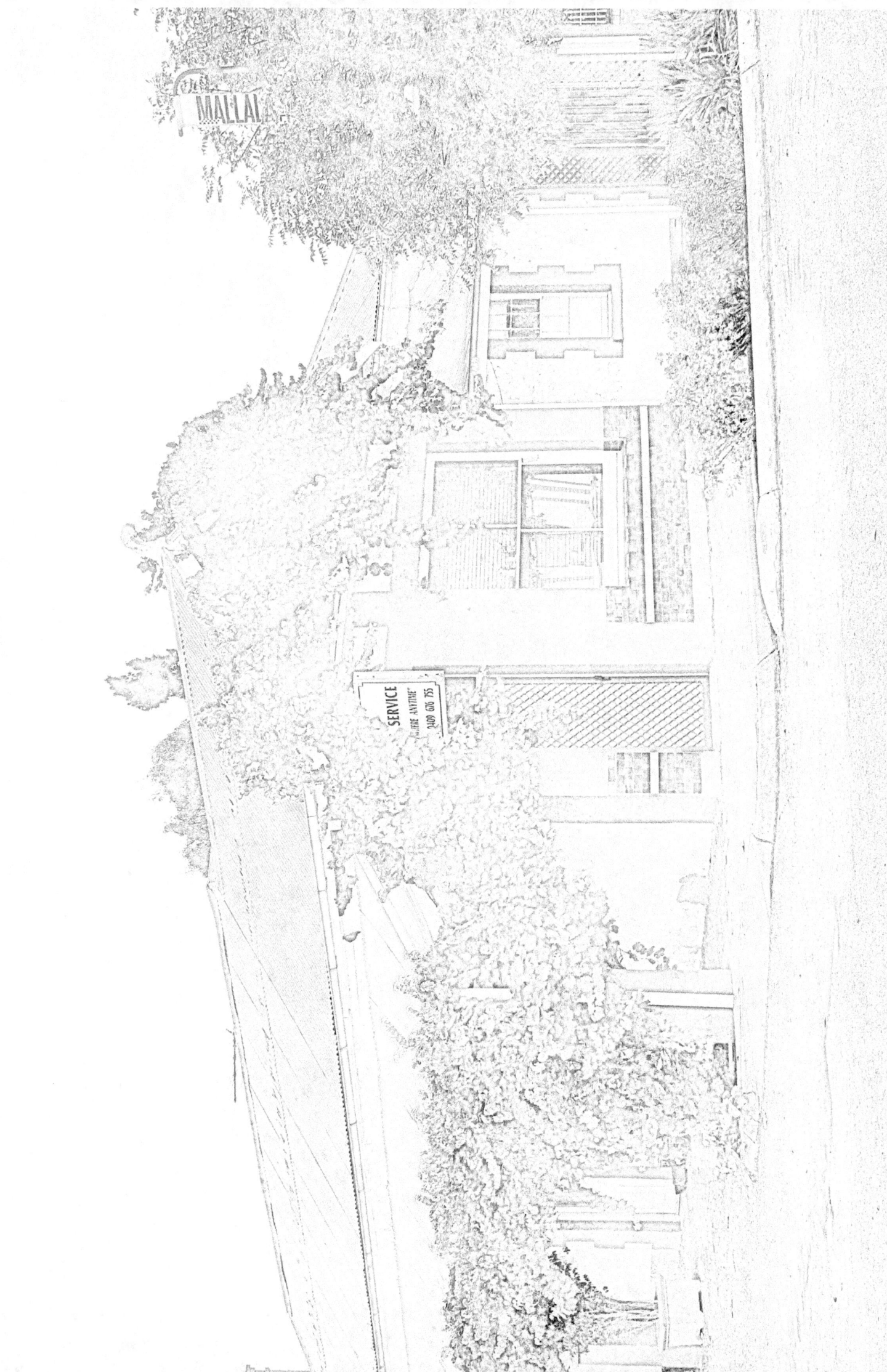

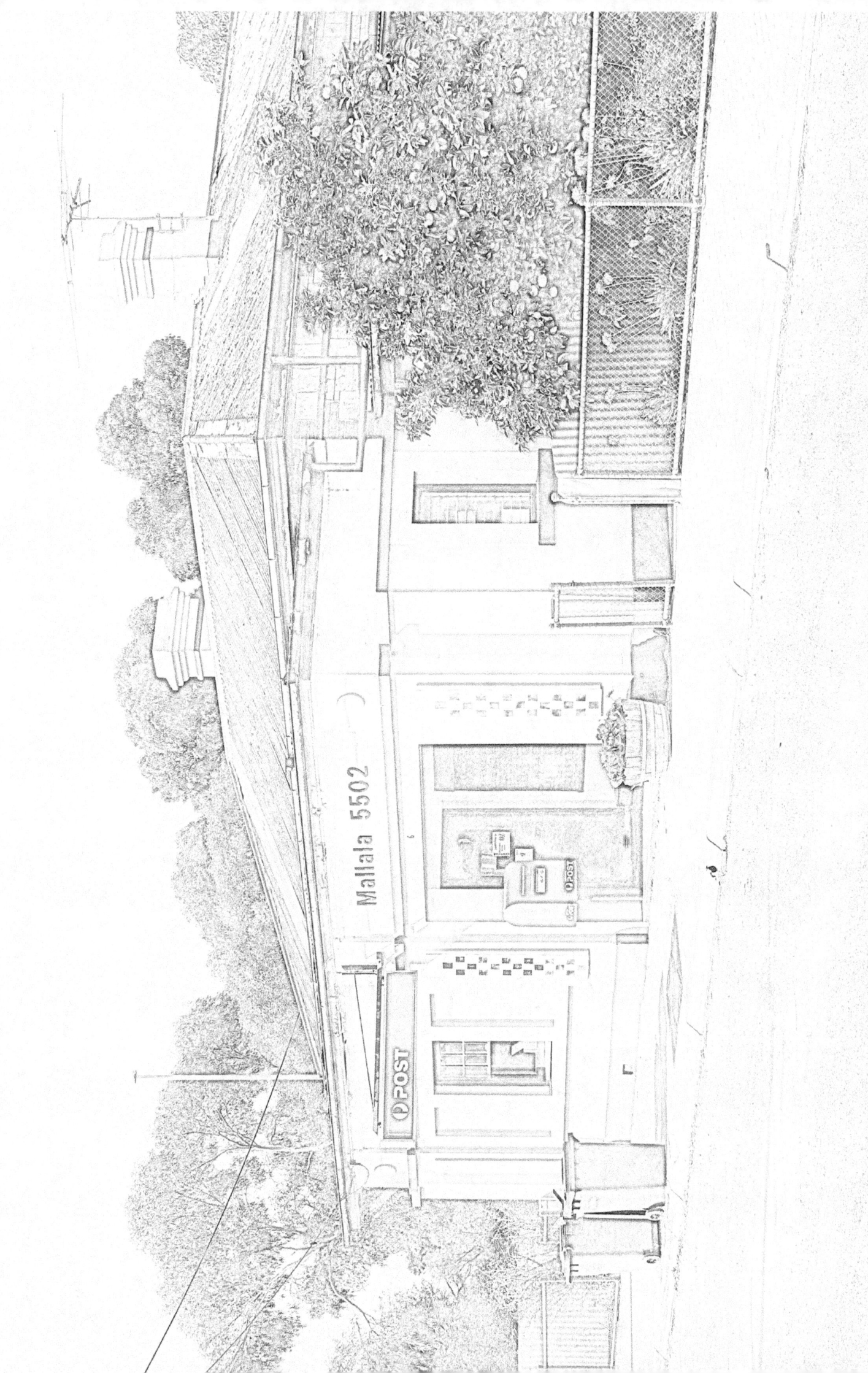

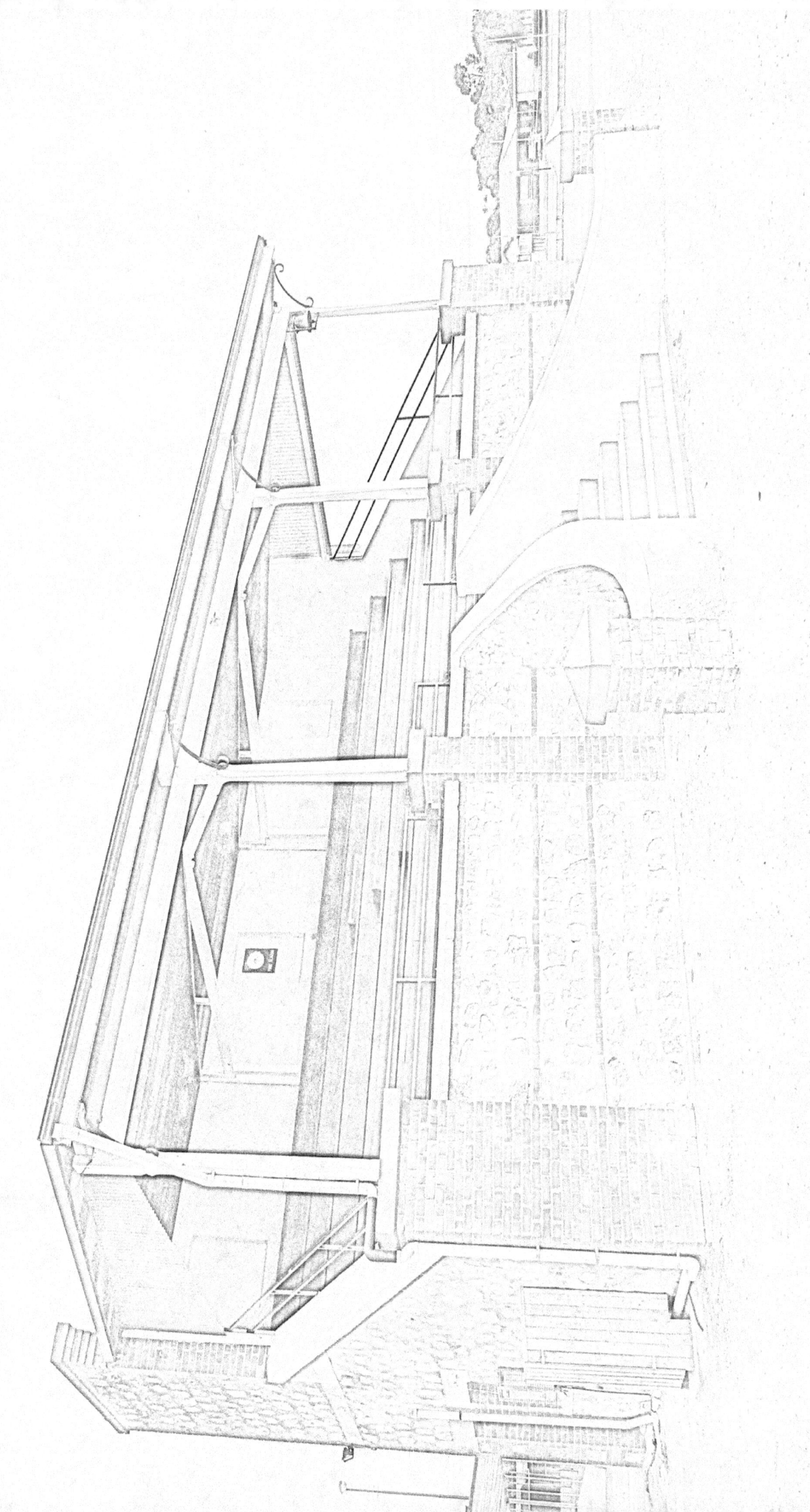

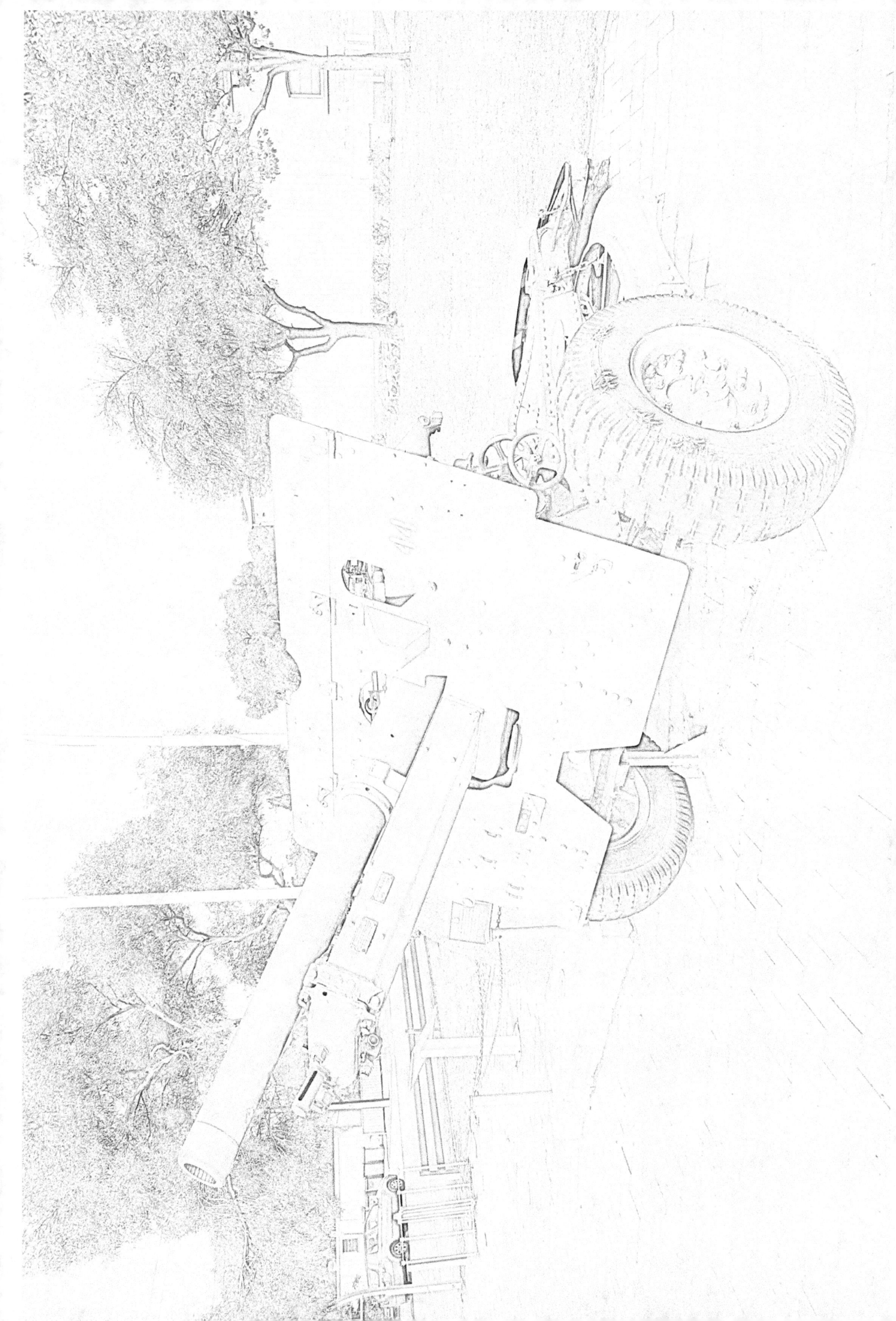

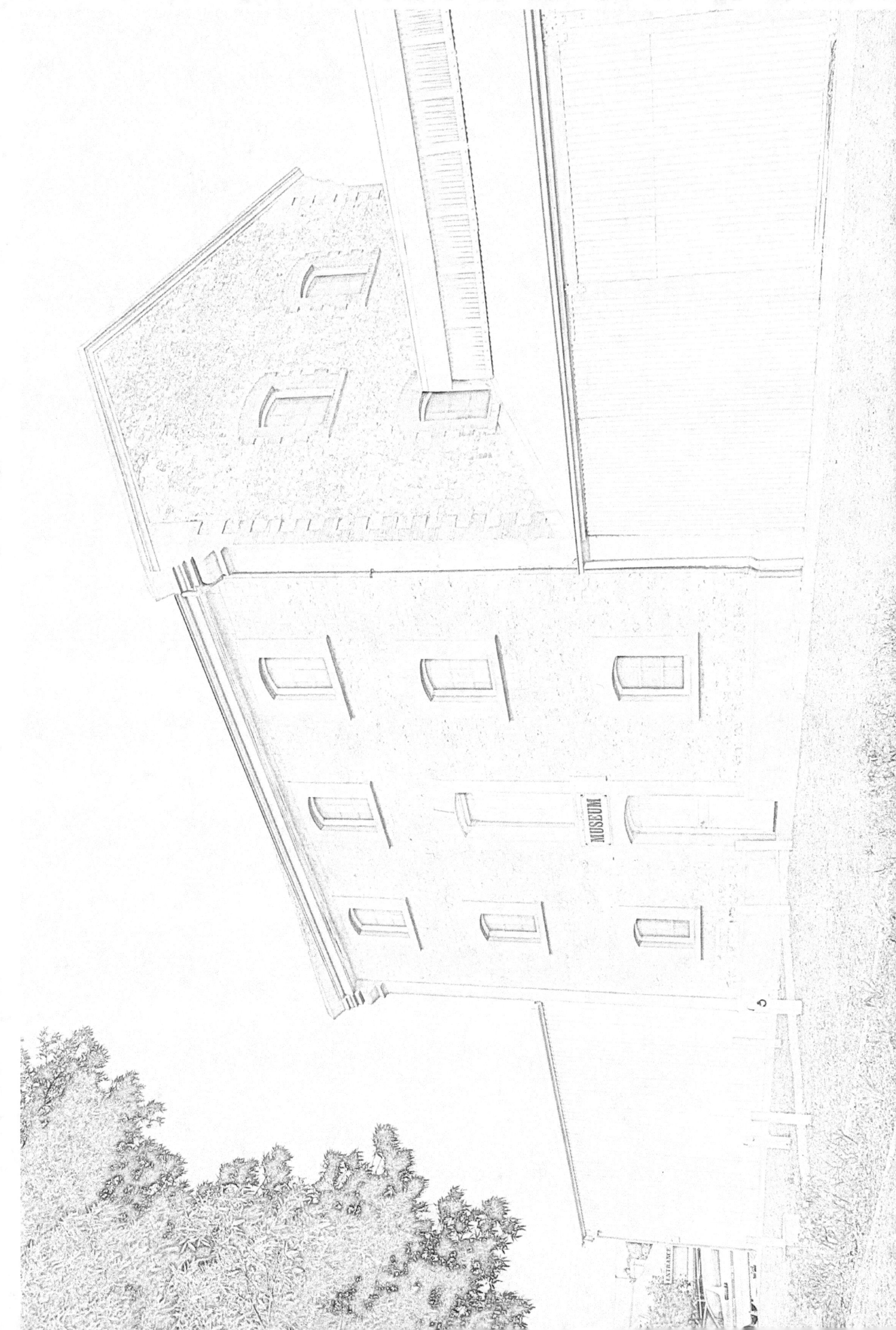

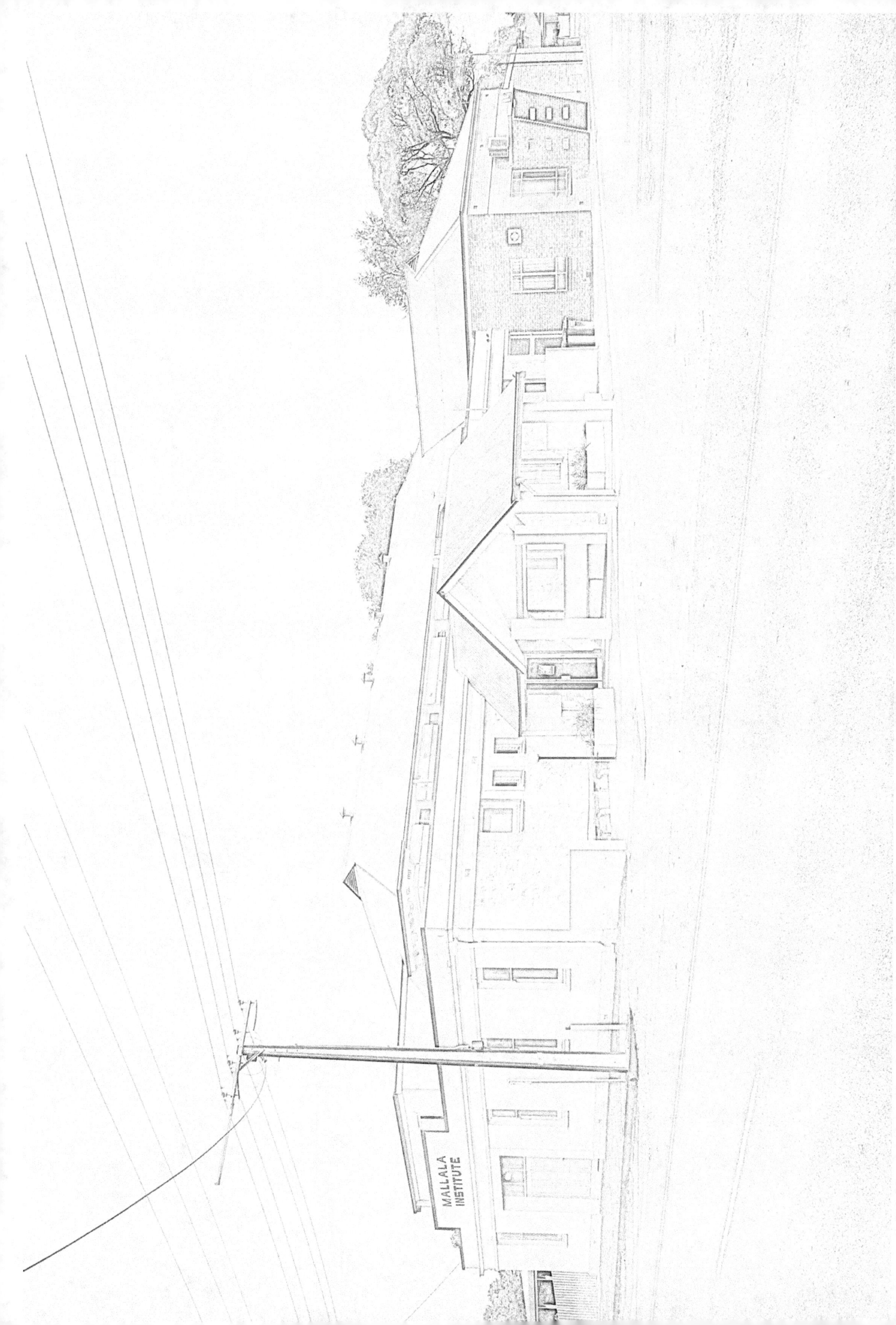

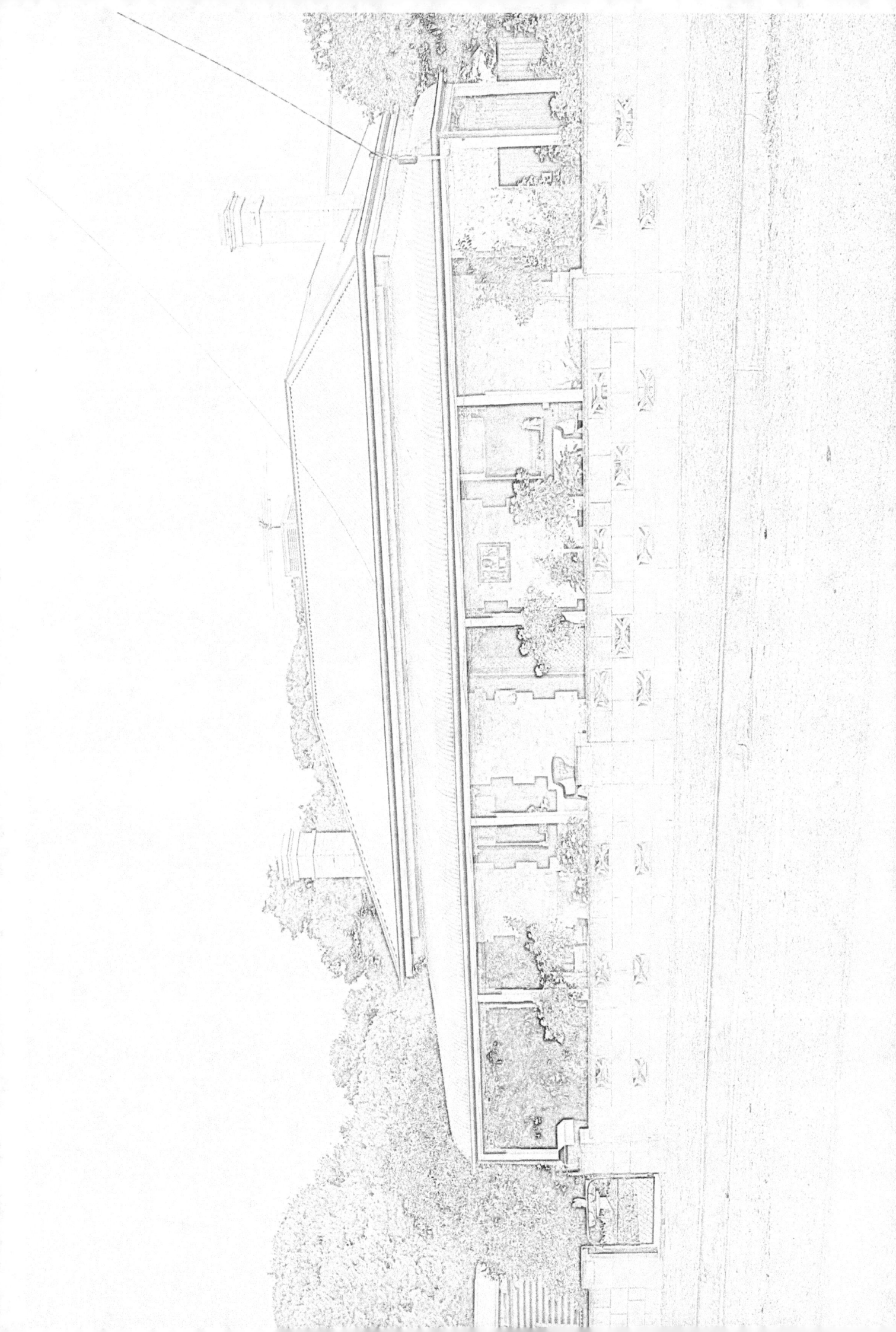

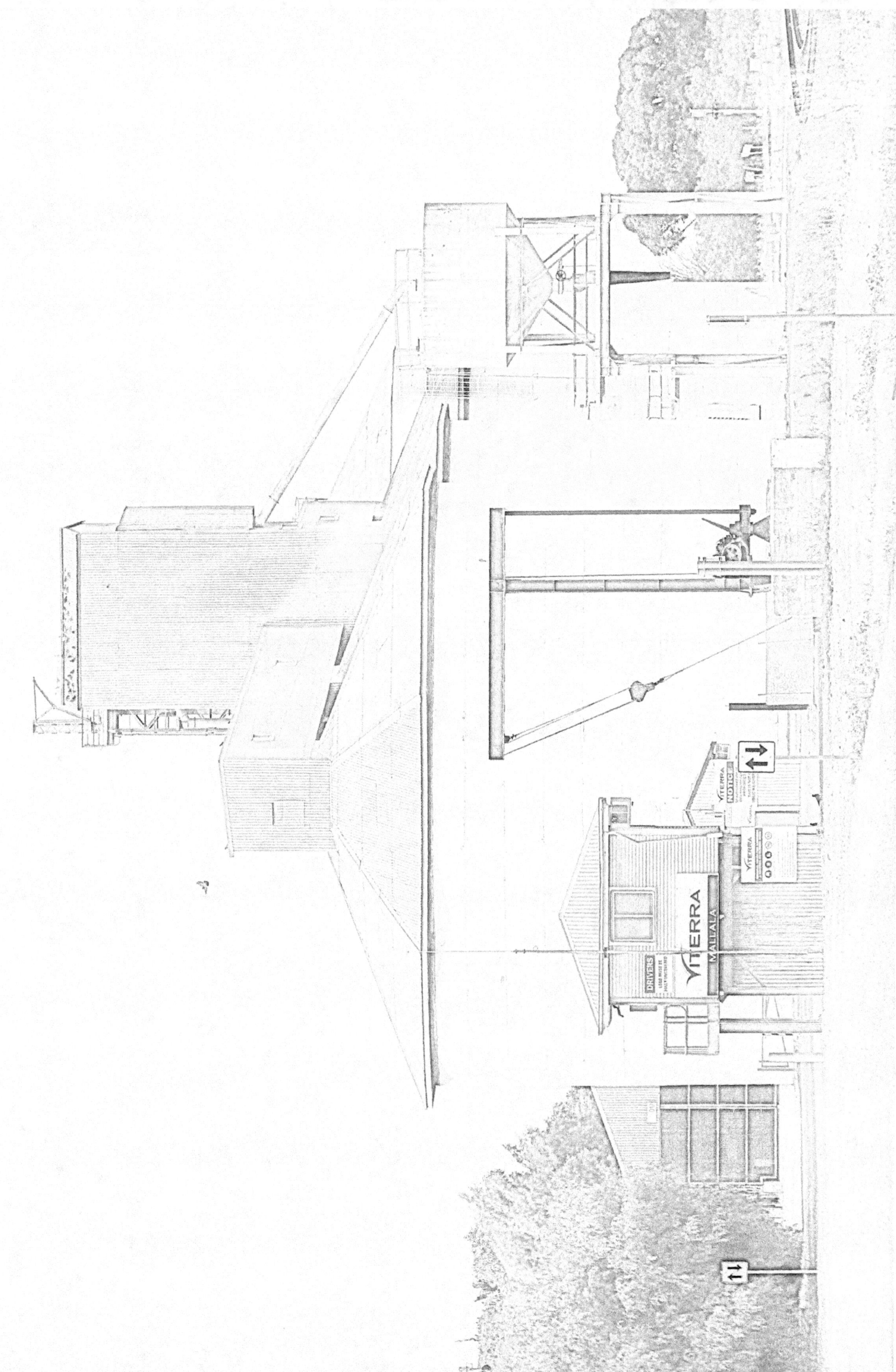

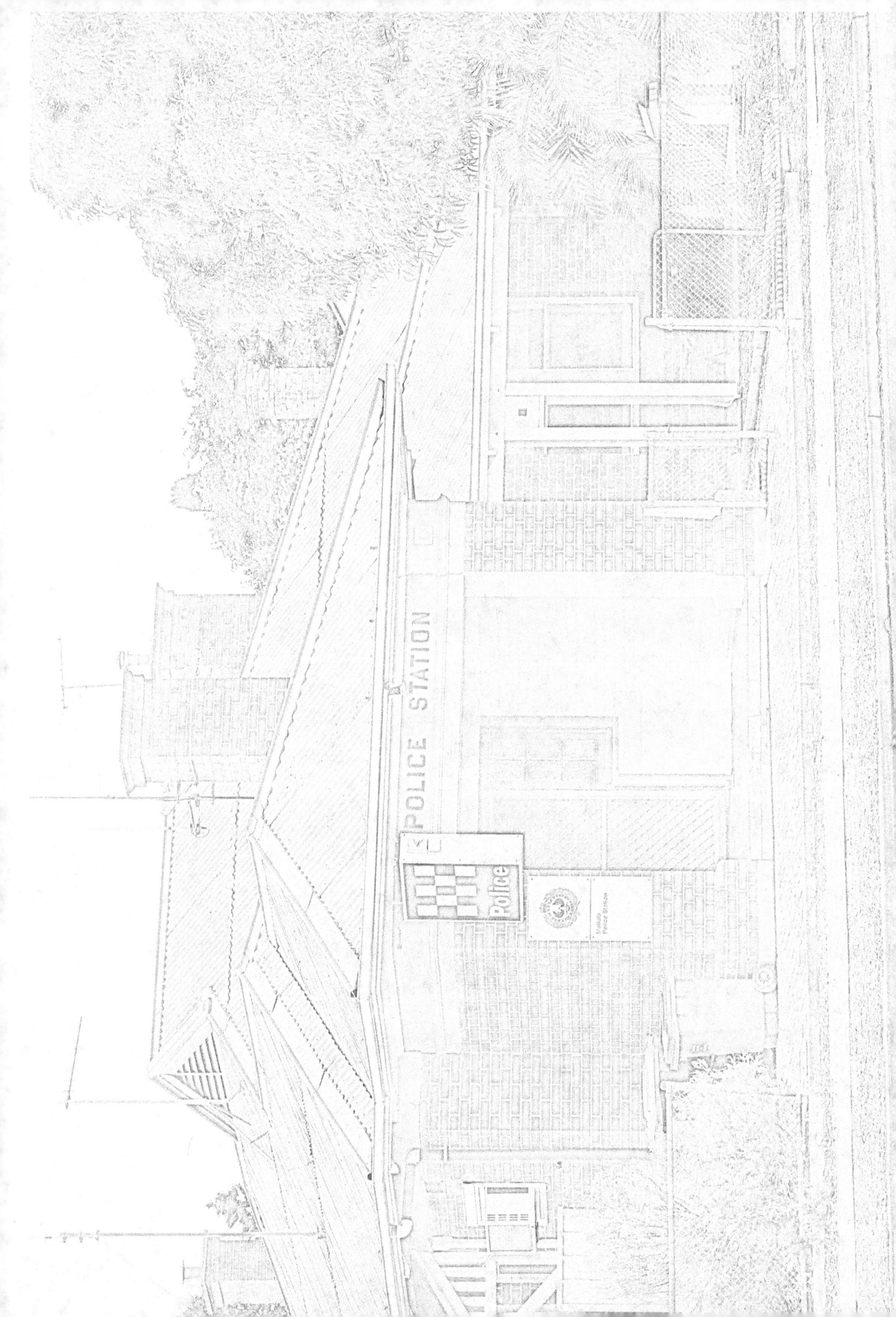

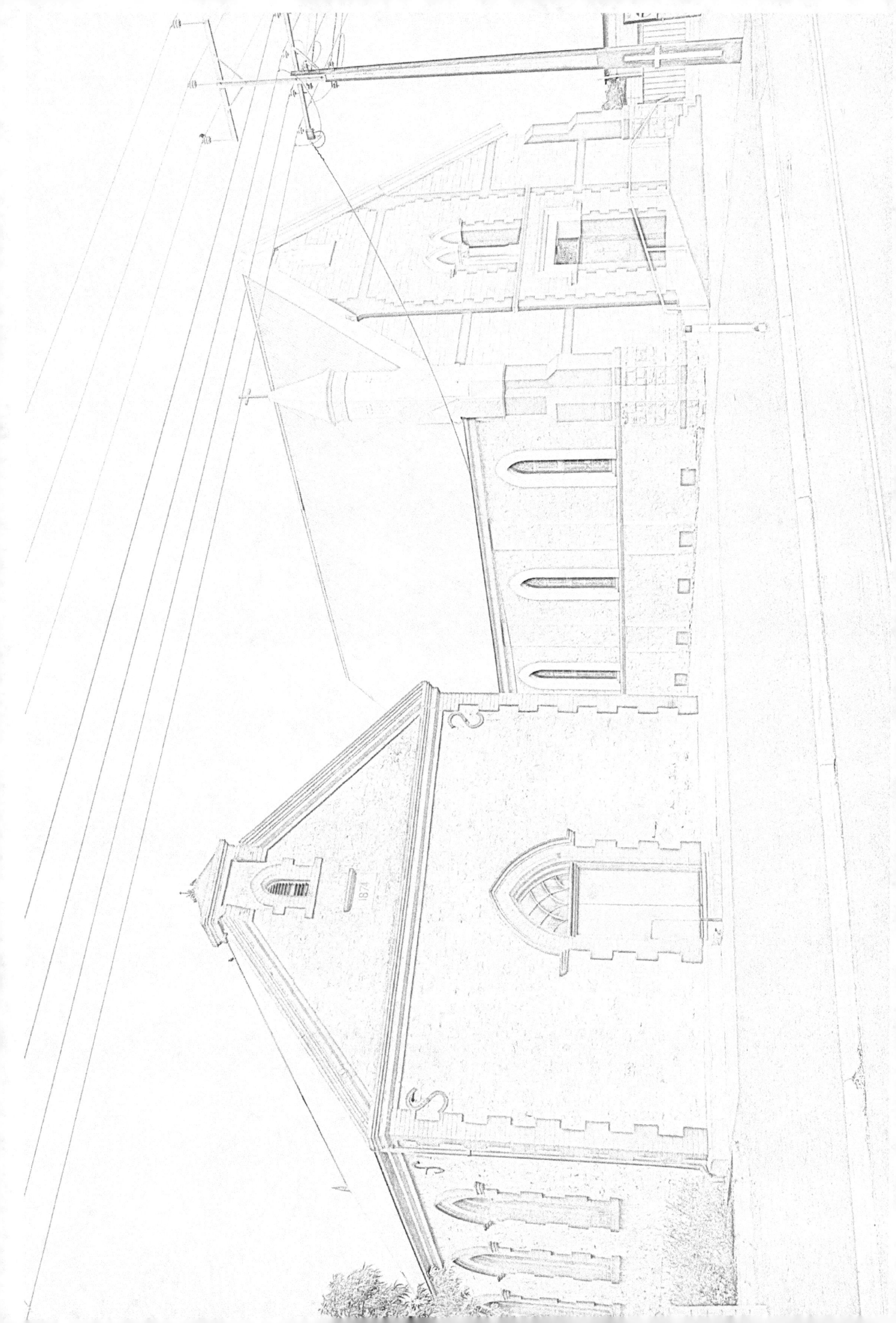

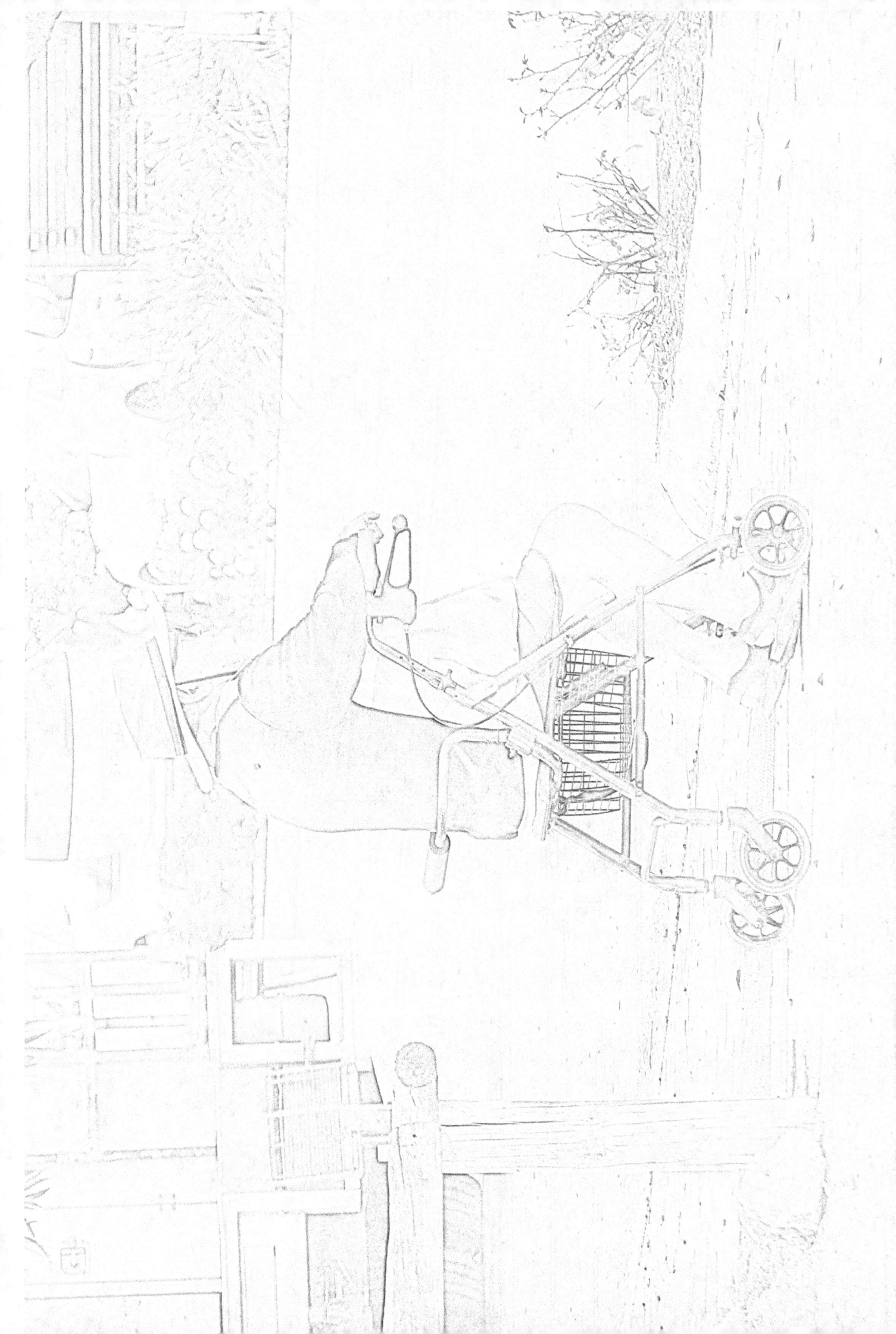

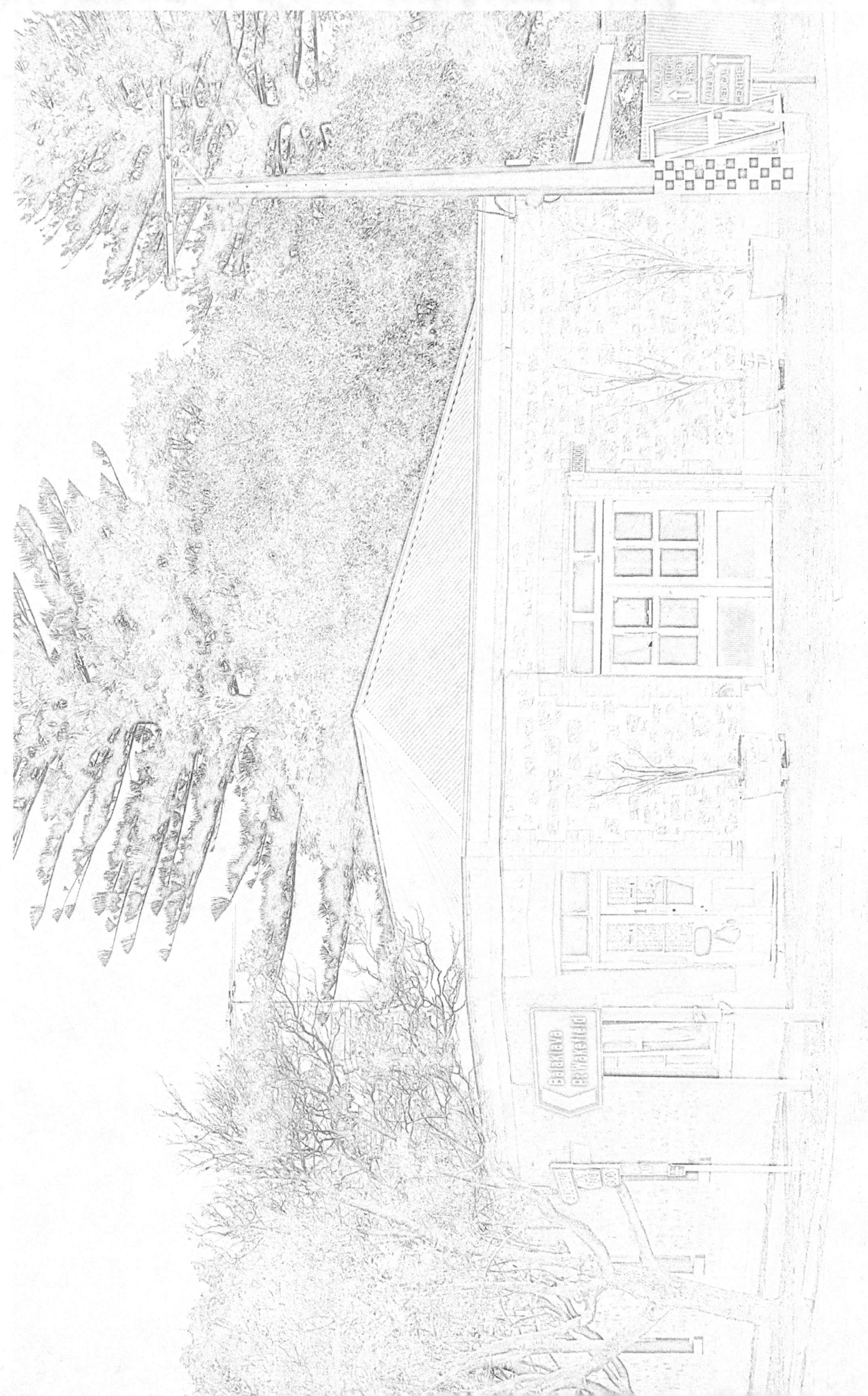

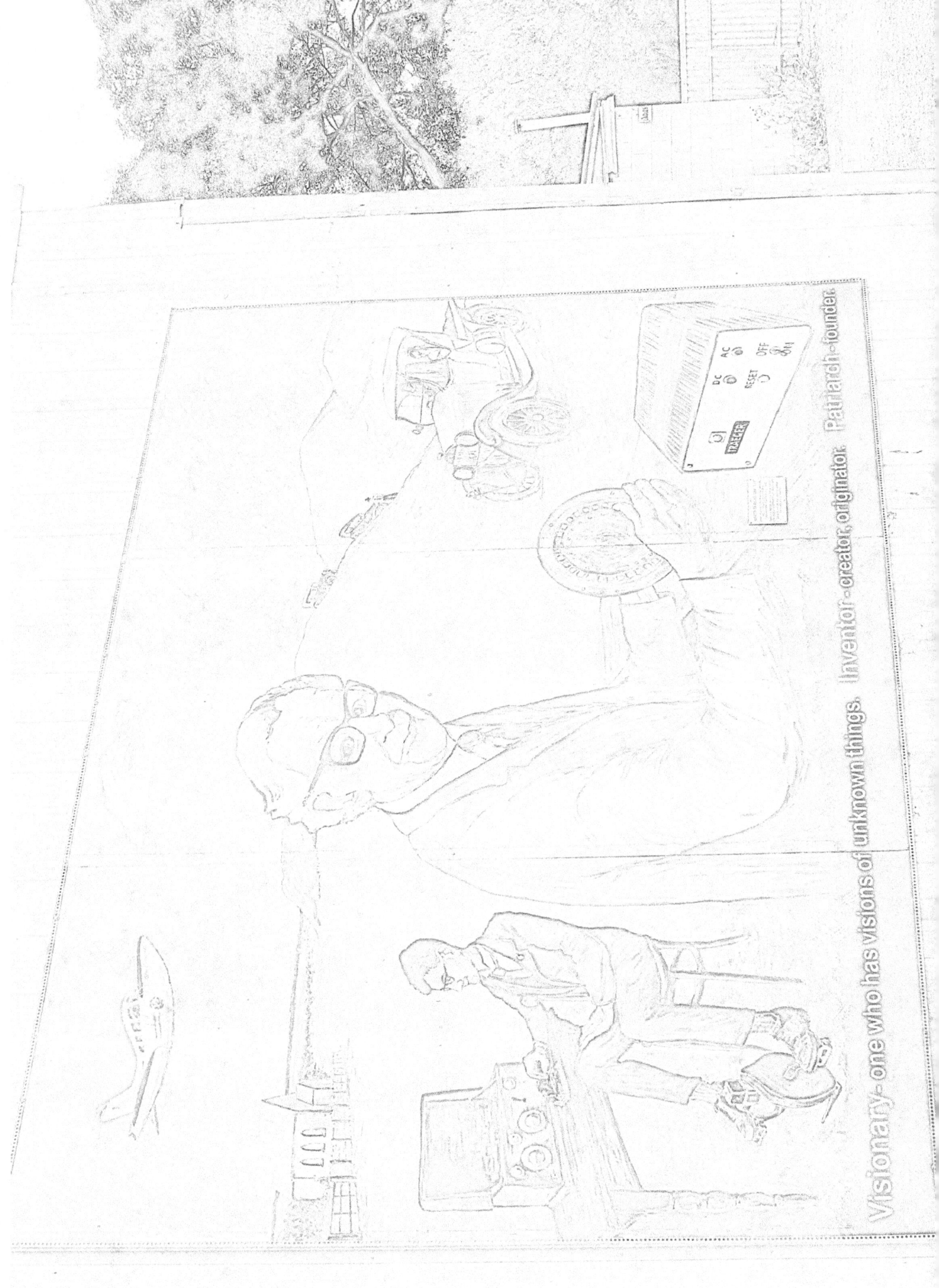

Visionary-one who has visions of unknown things. Inventor-creator, originator. Patriarch-founder.

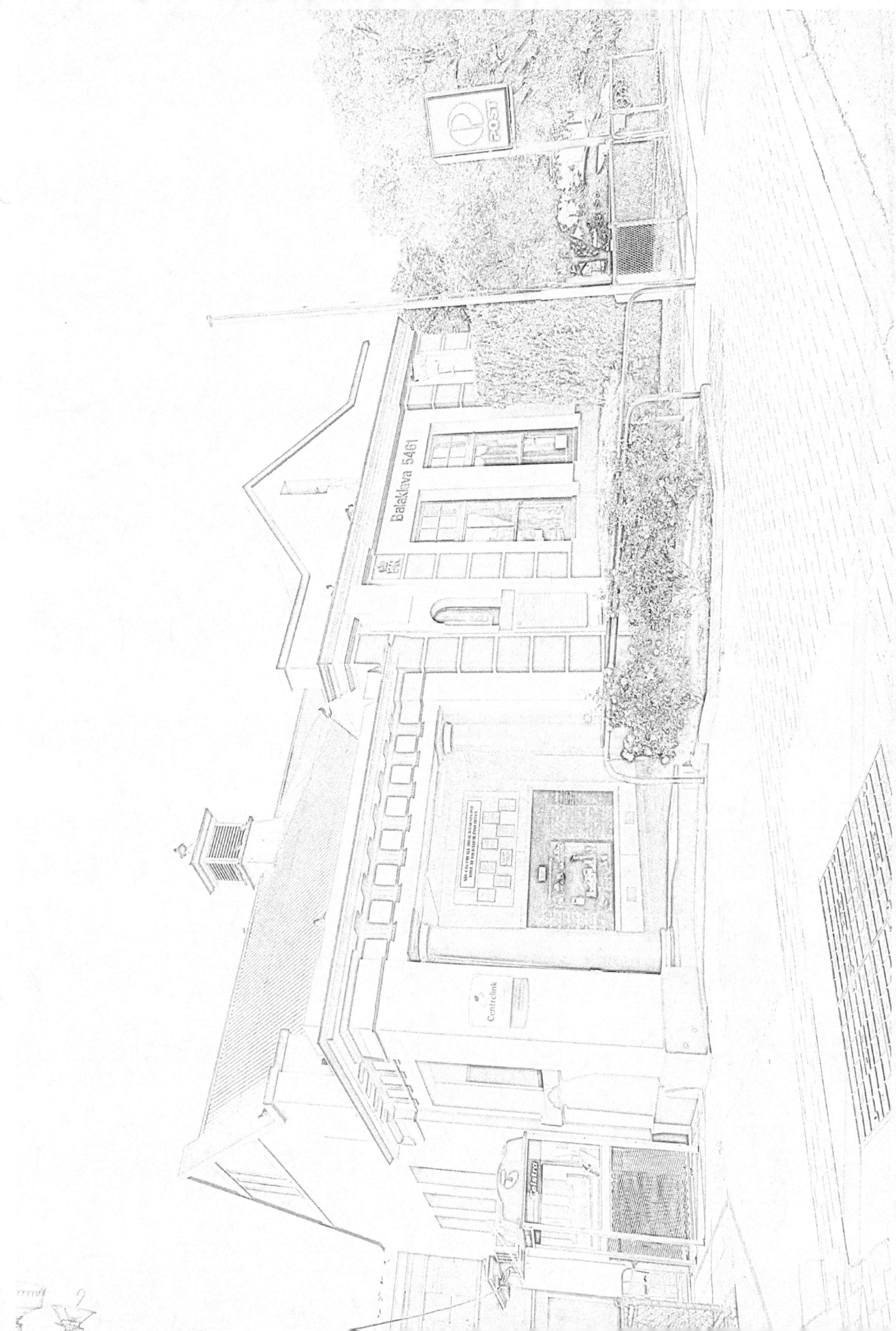

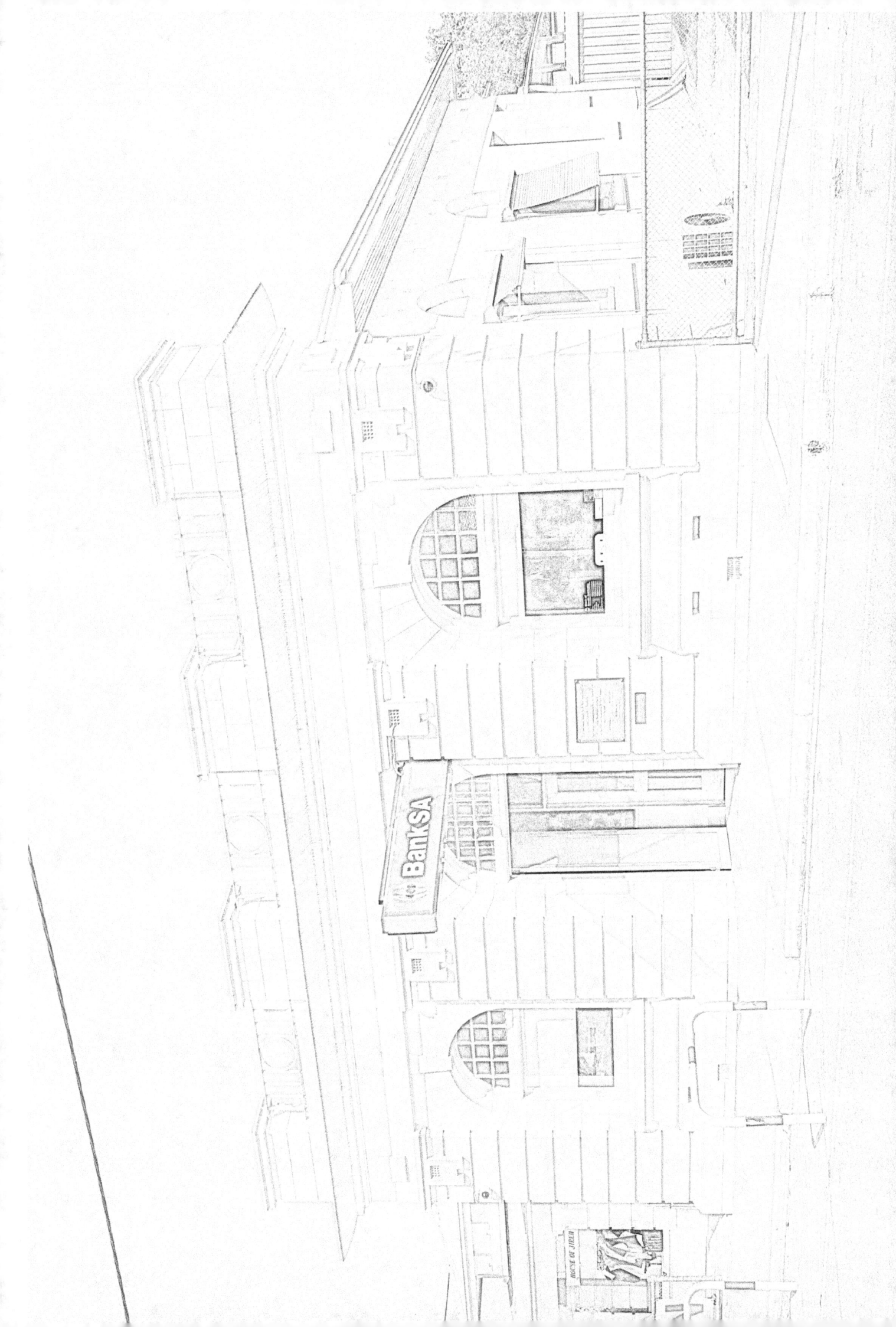

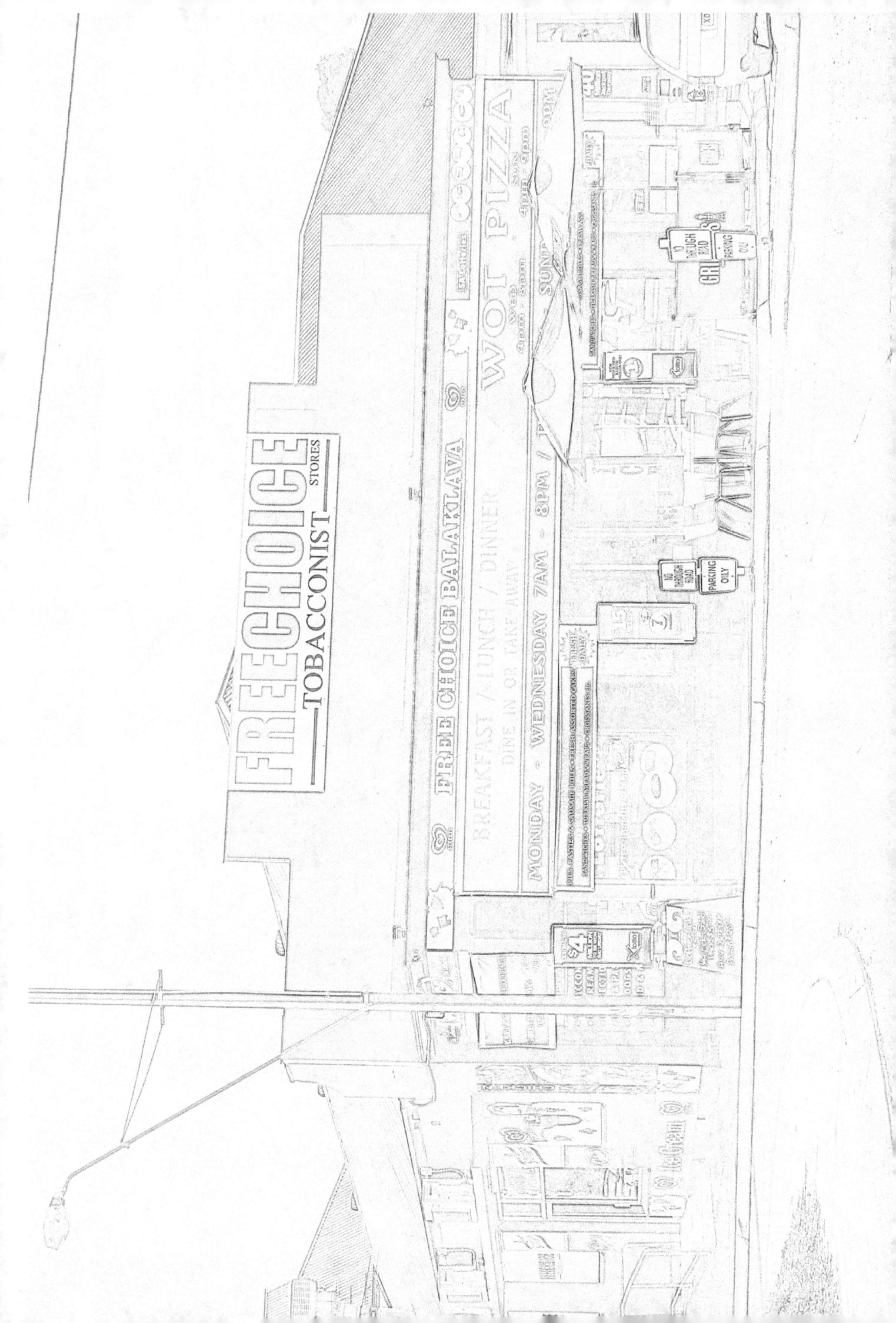

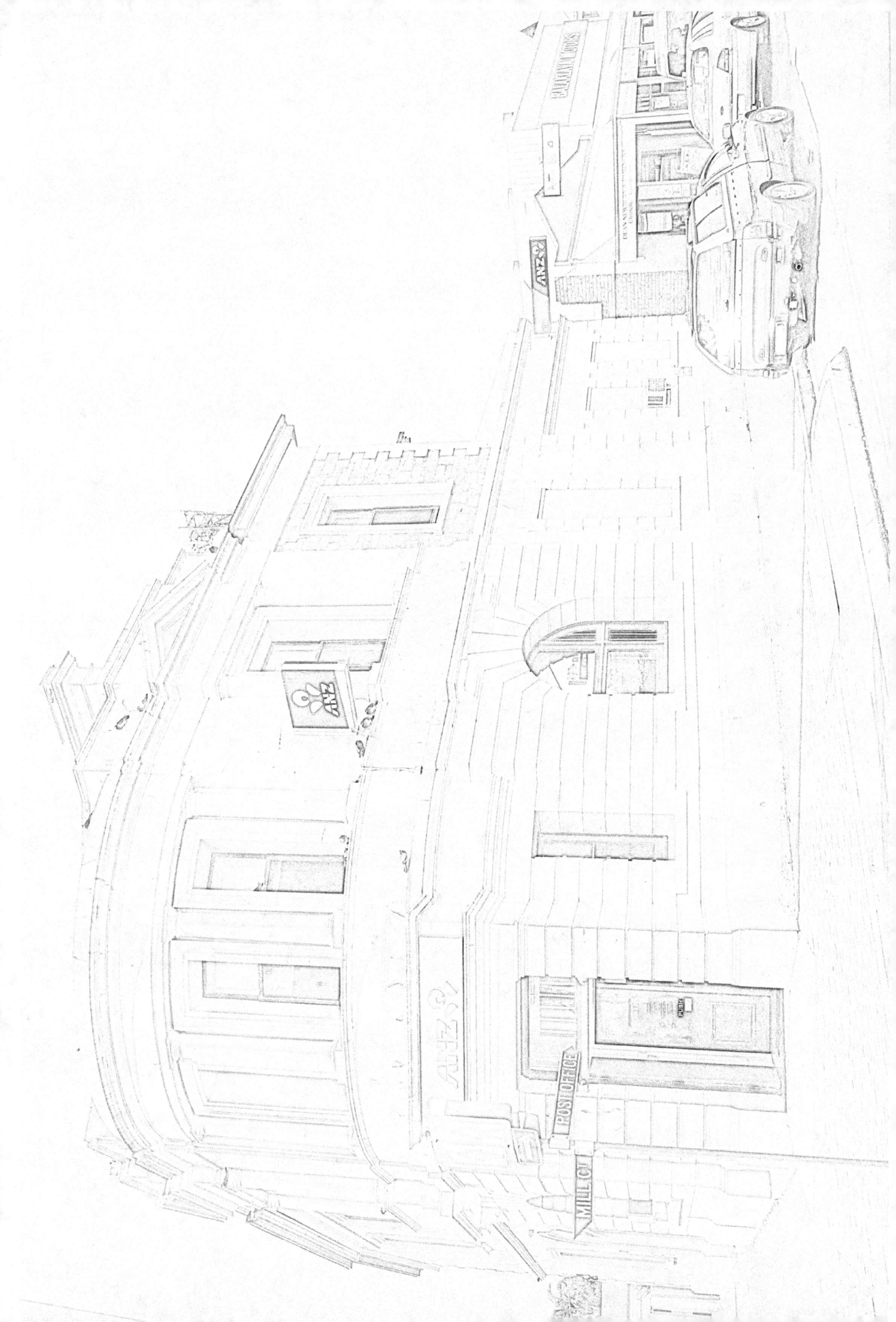

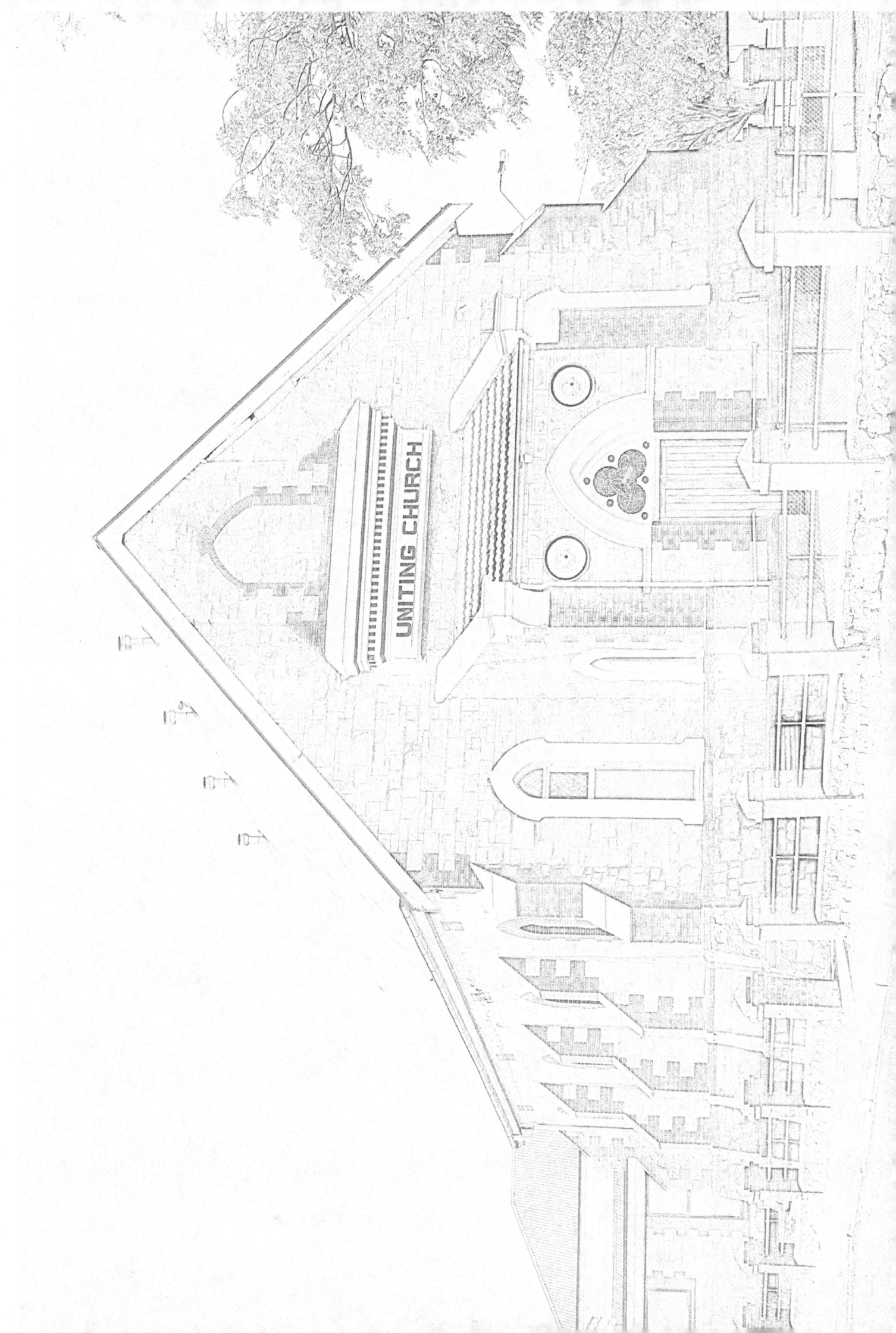

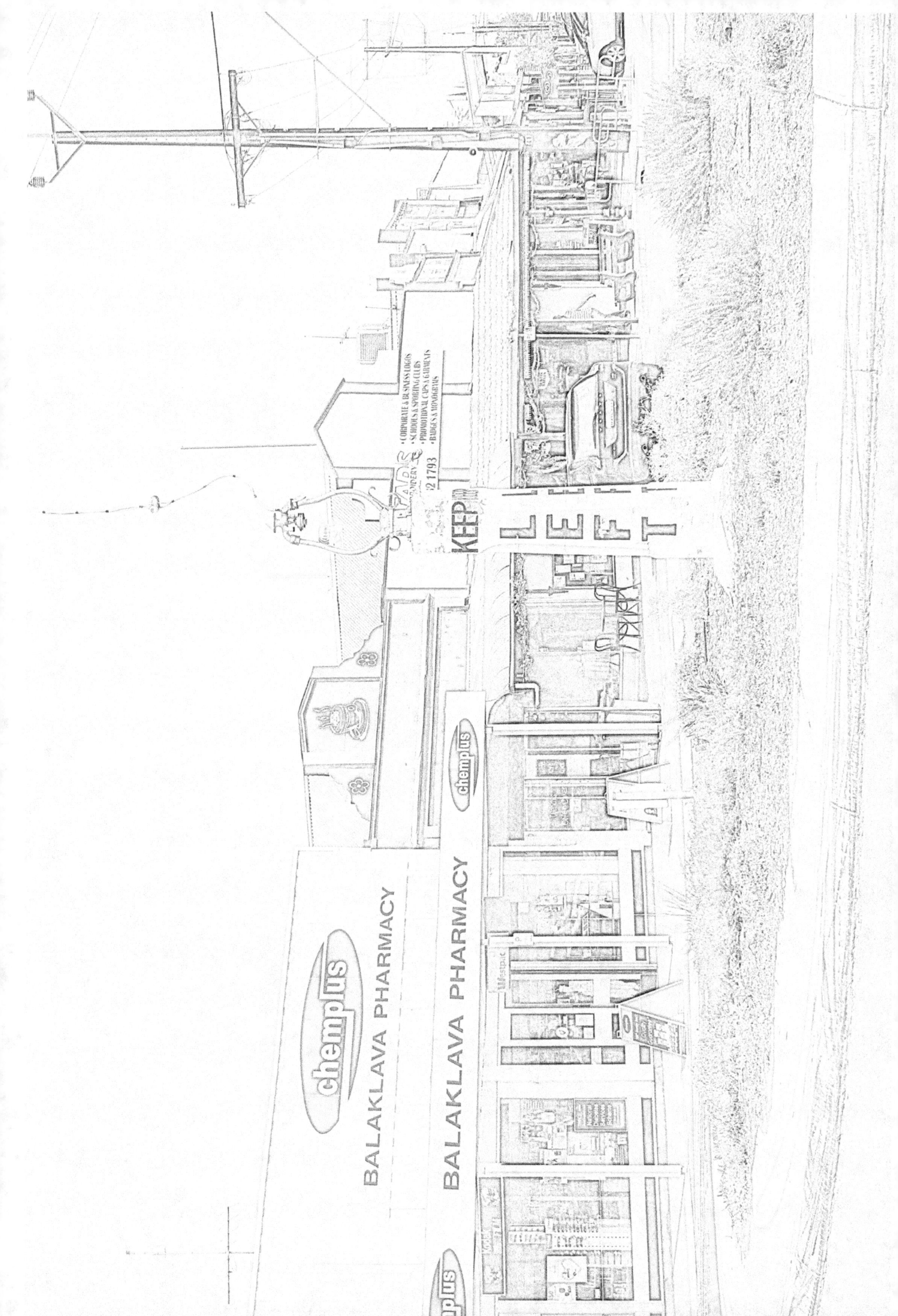

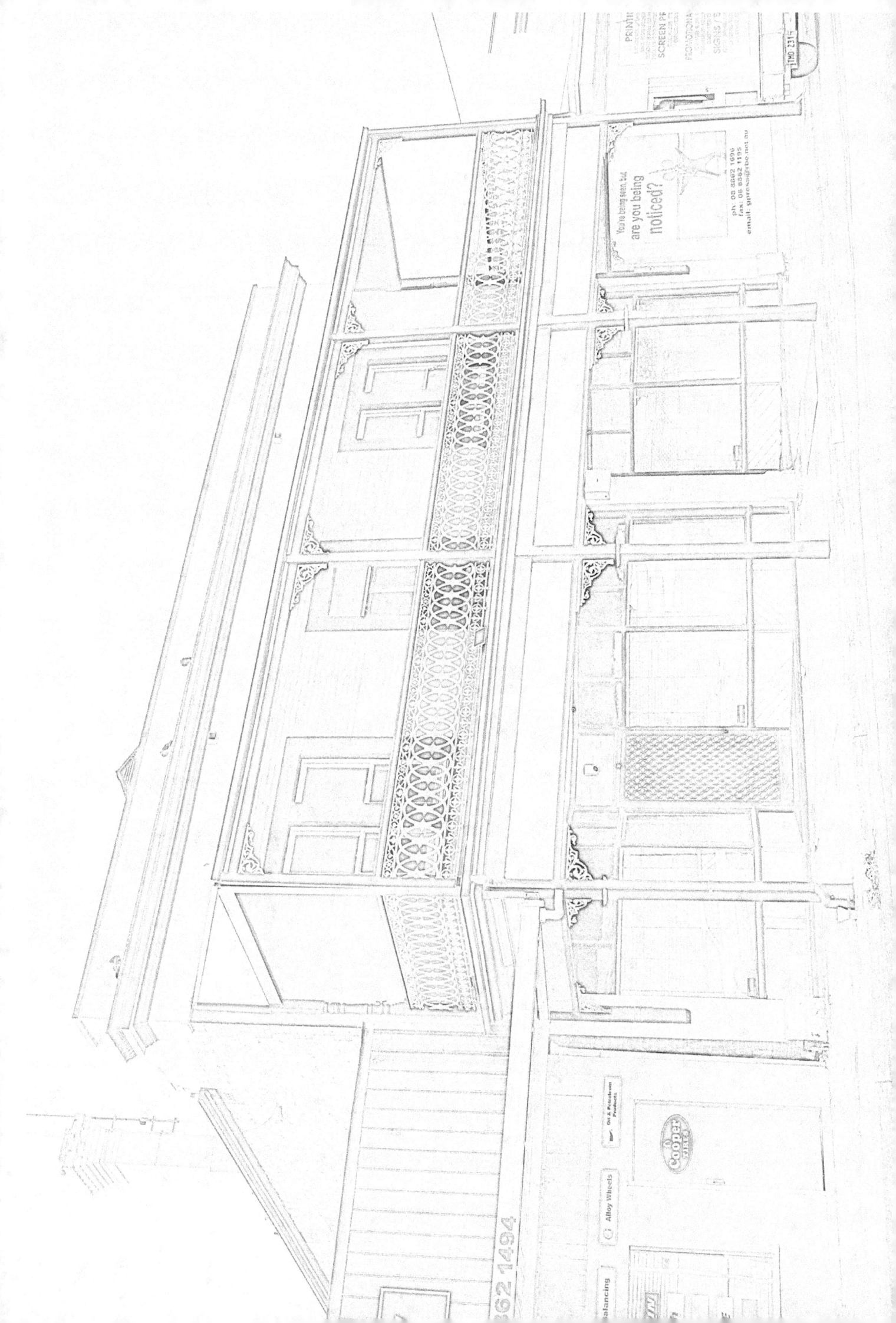

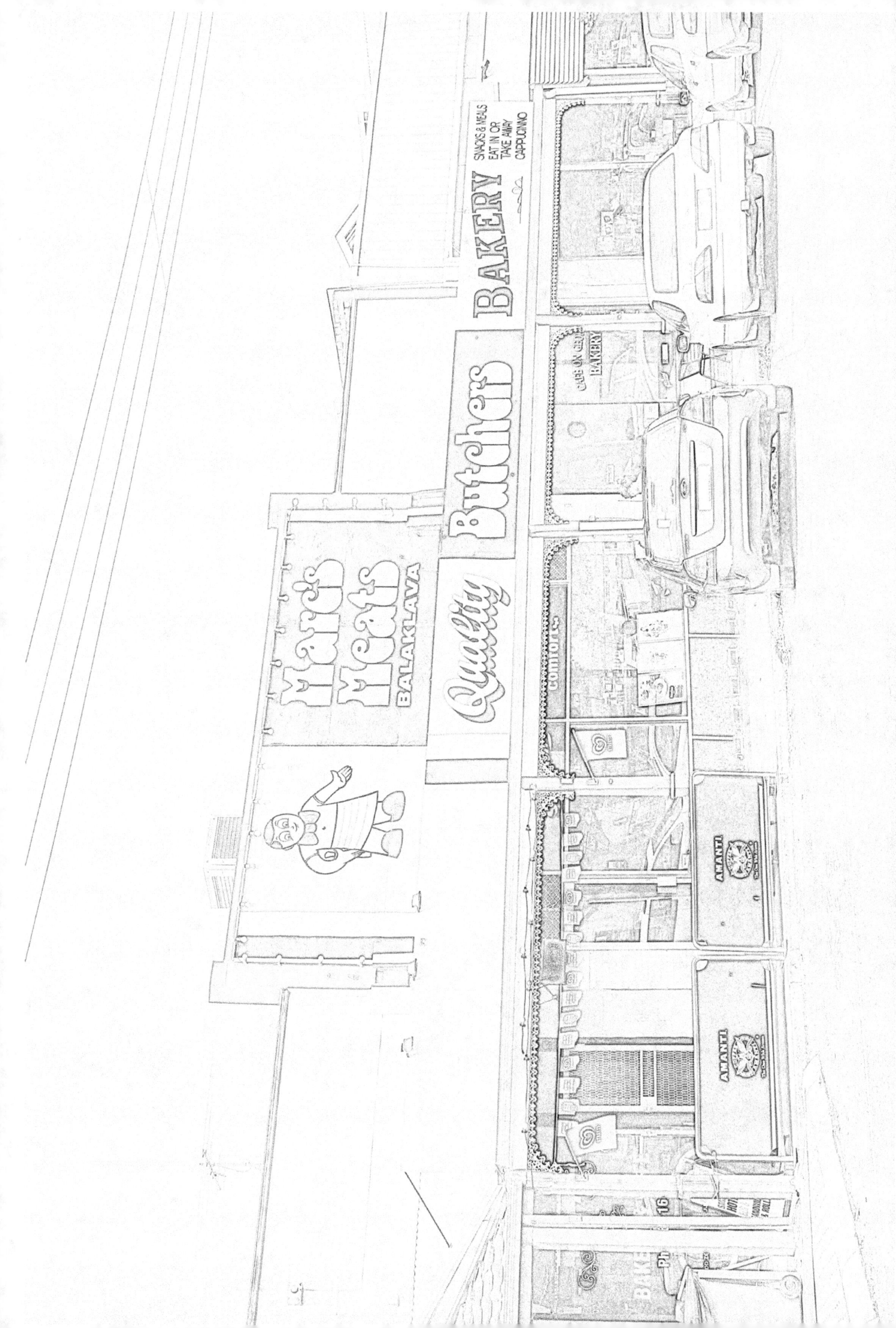

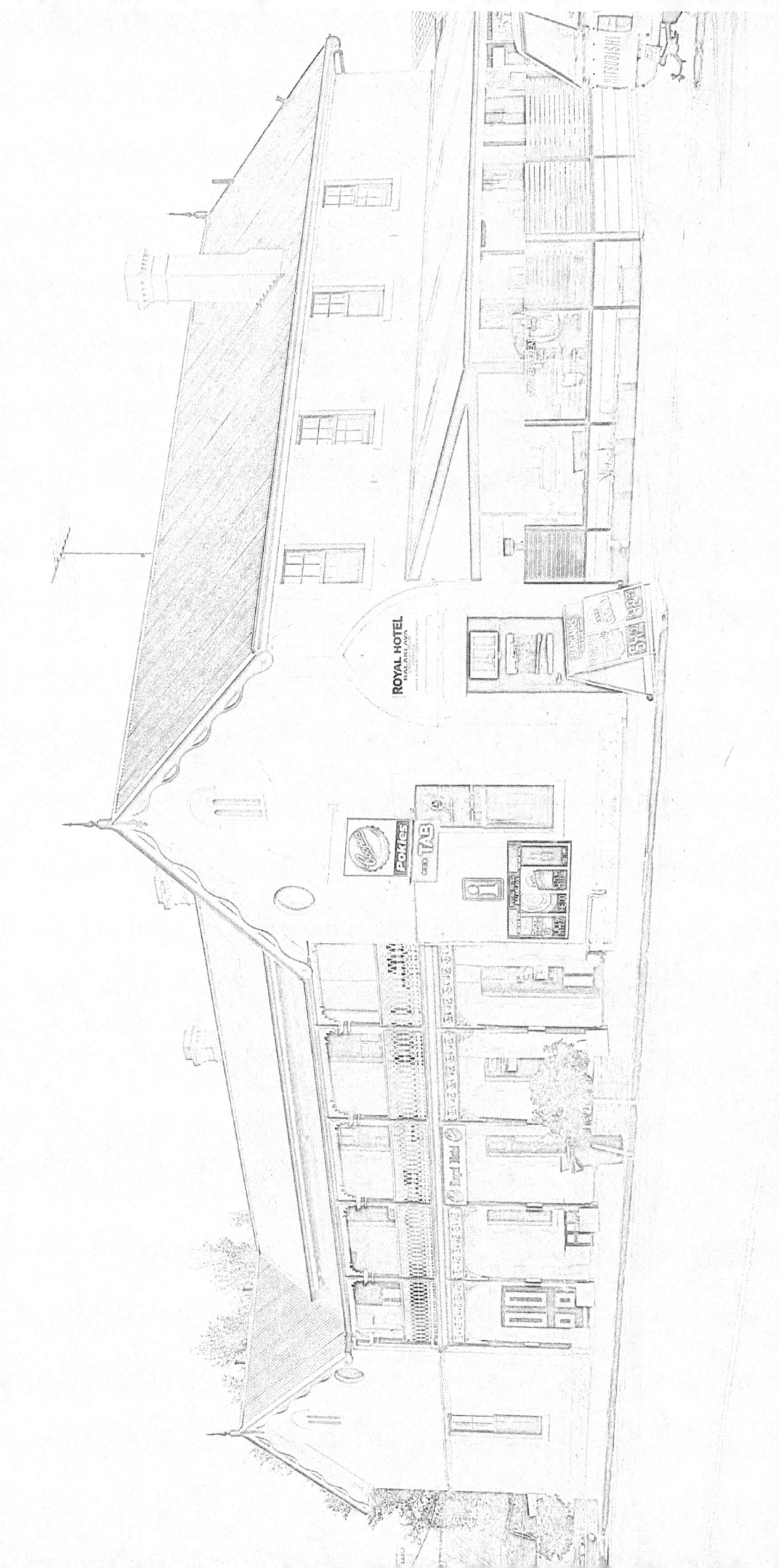

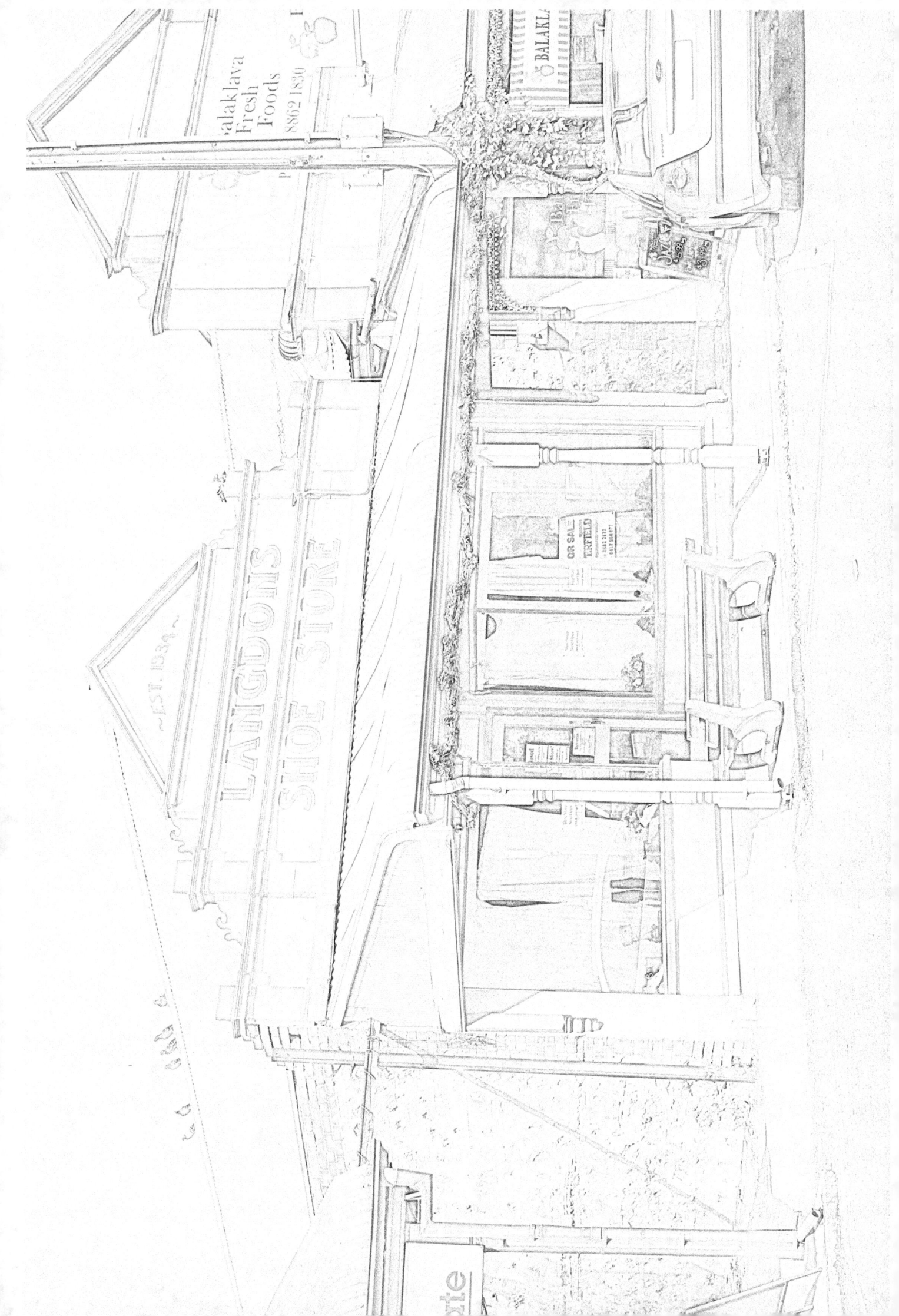

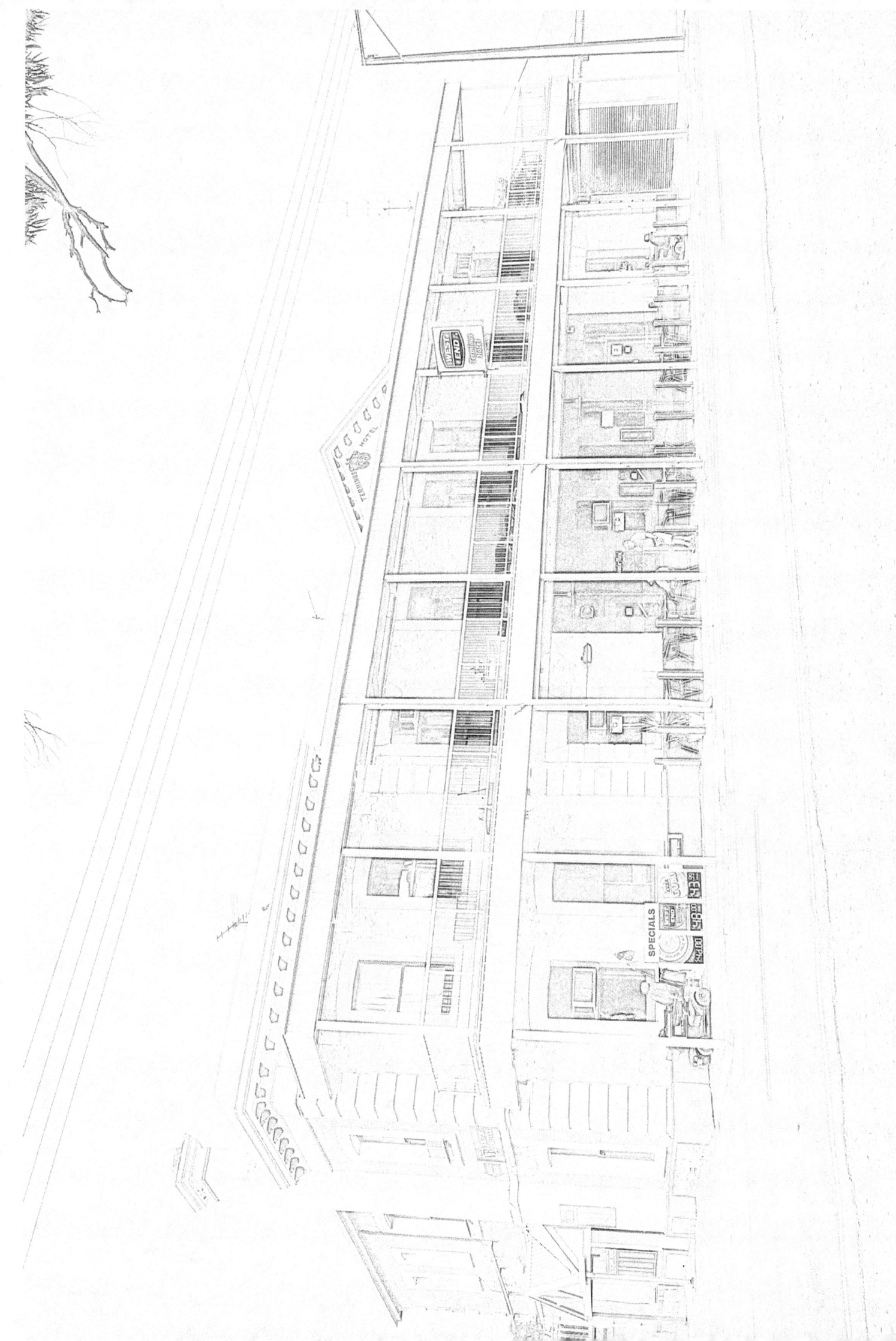

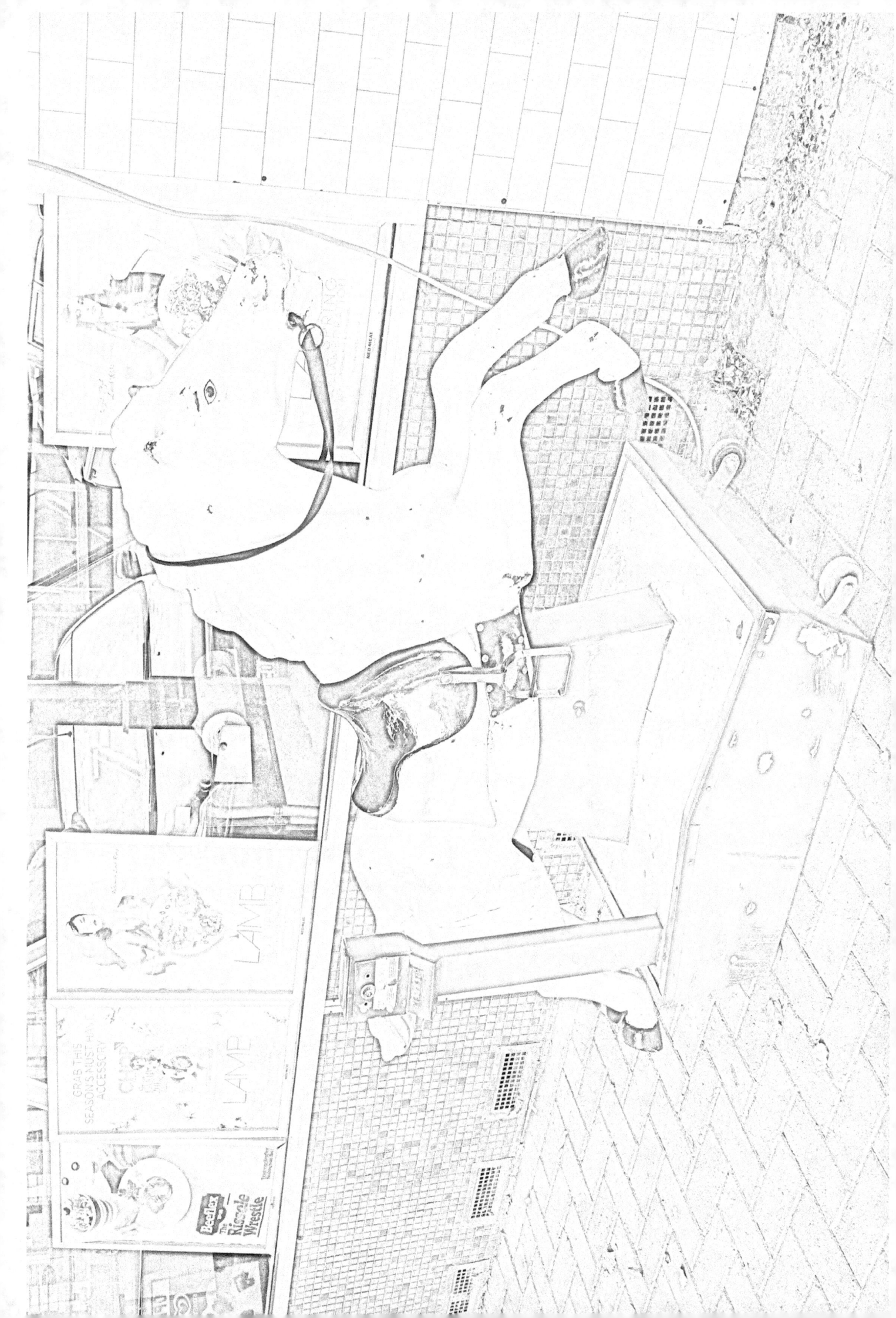

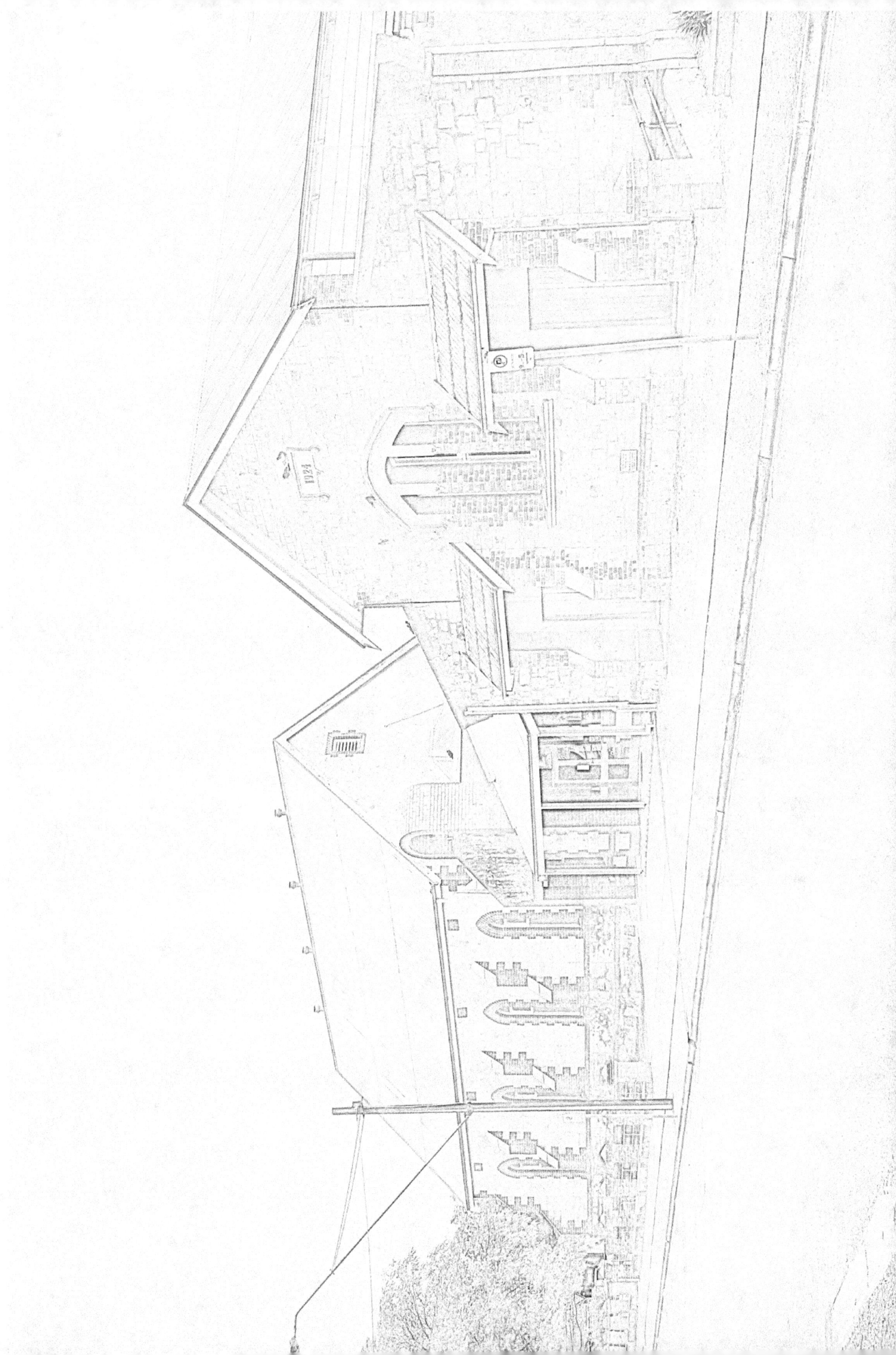

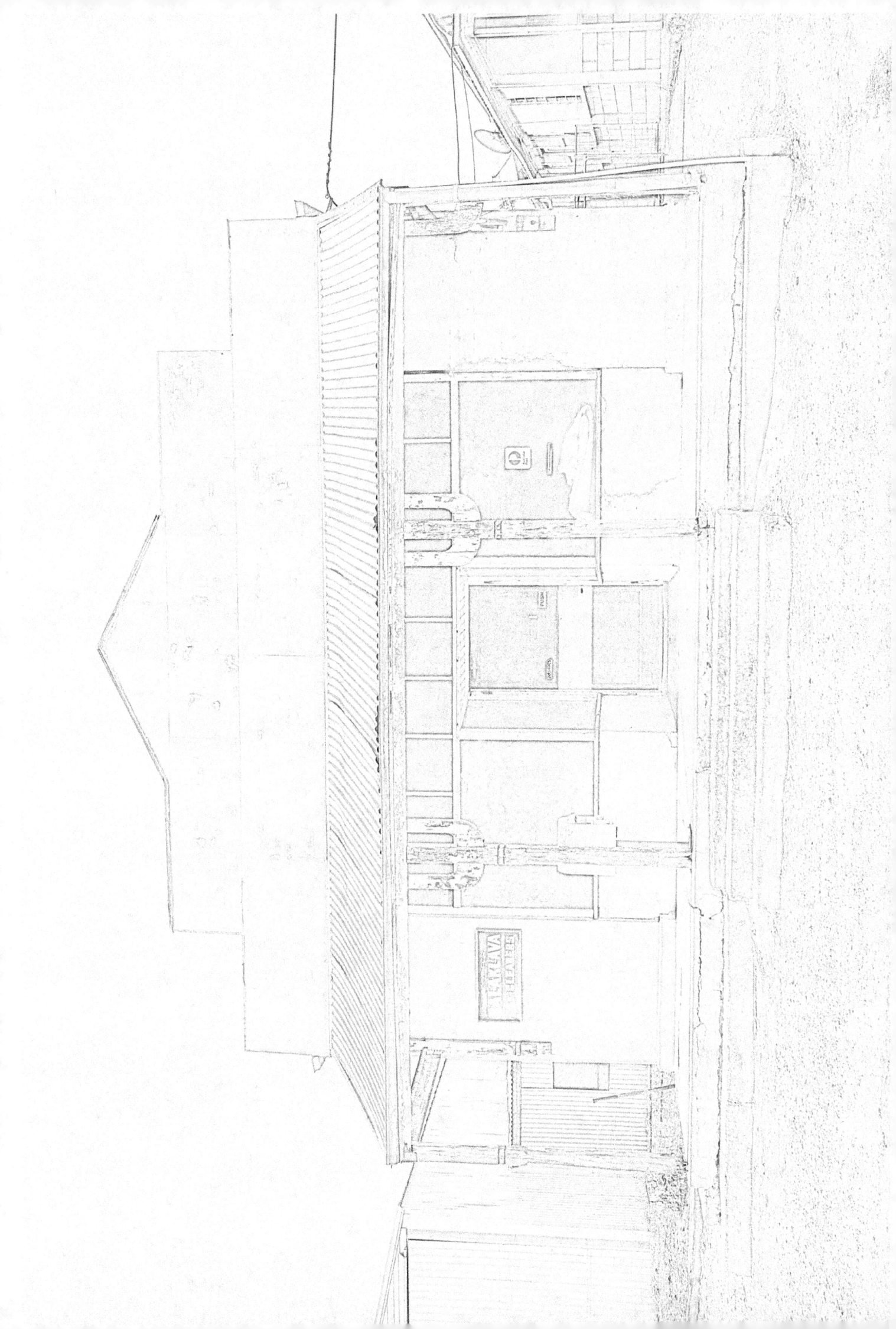

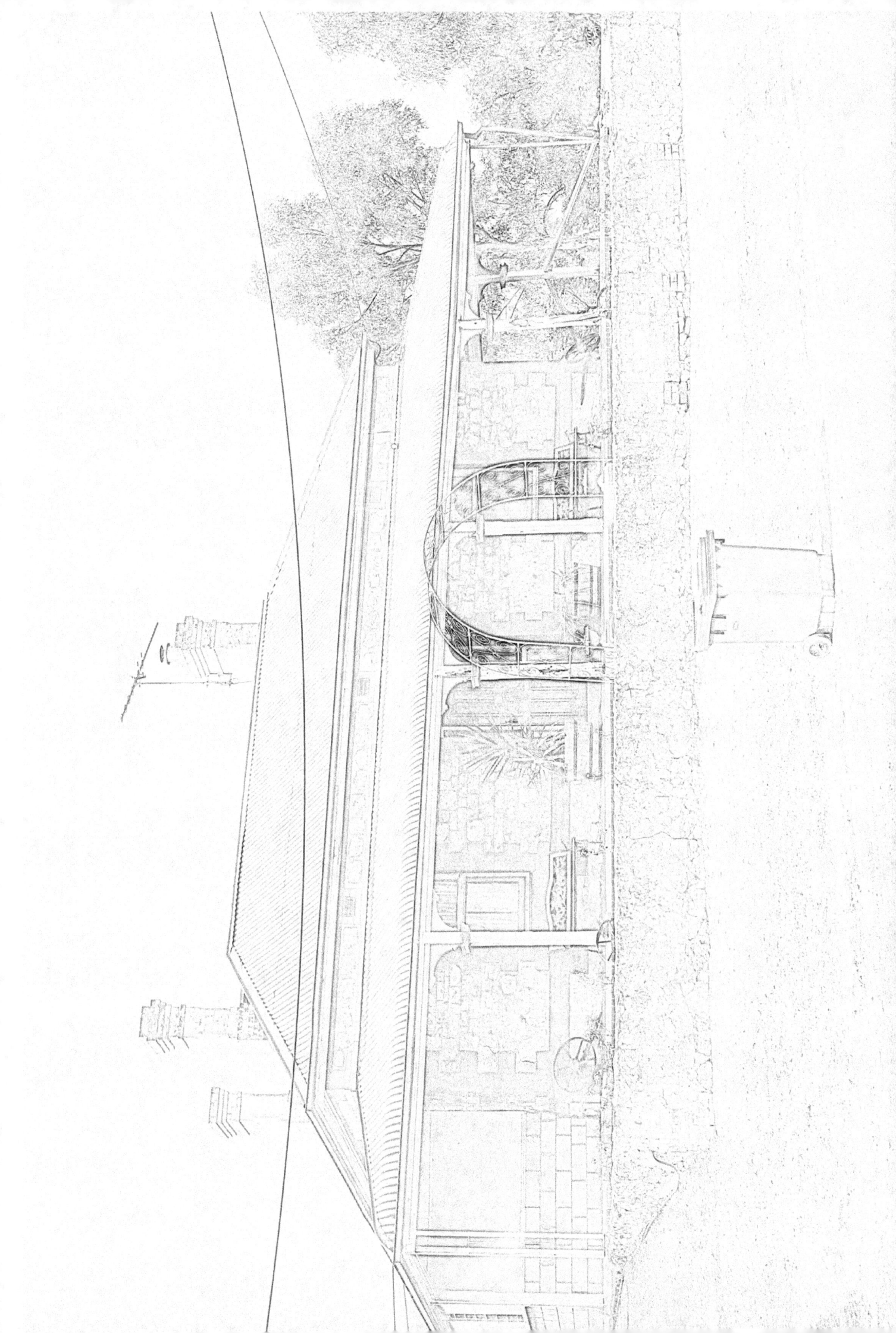

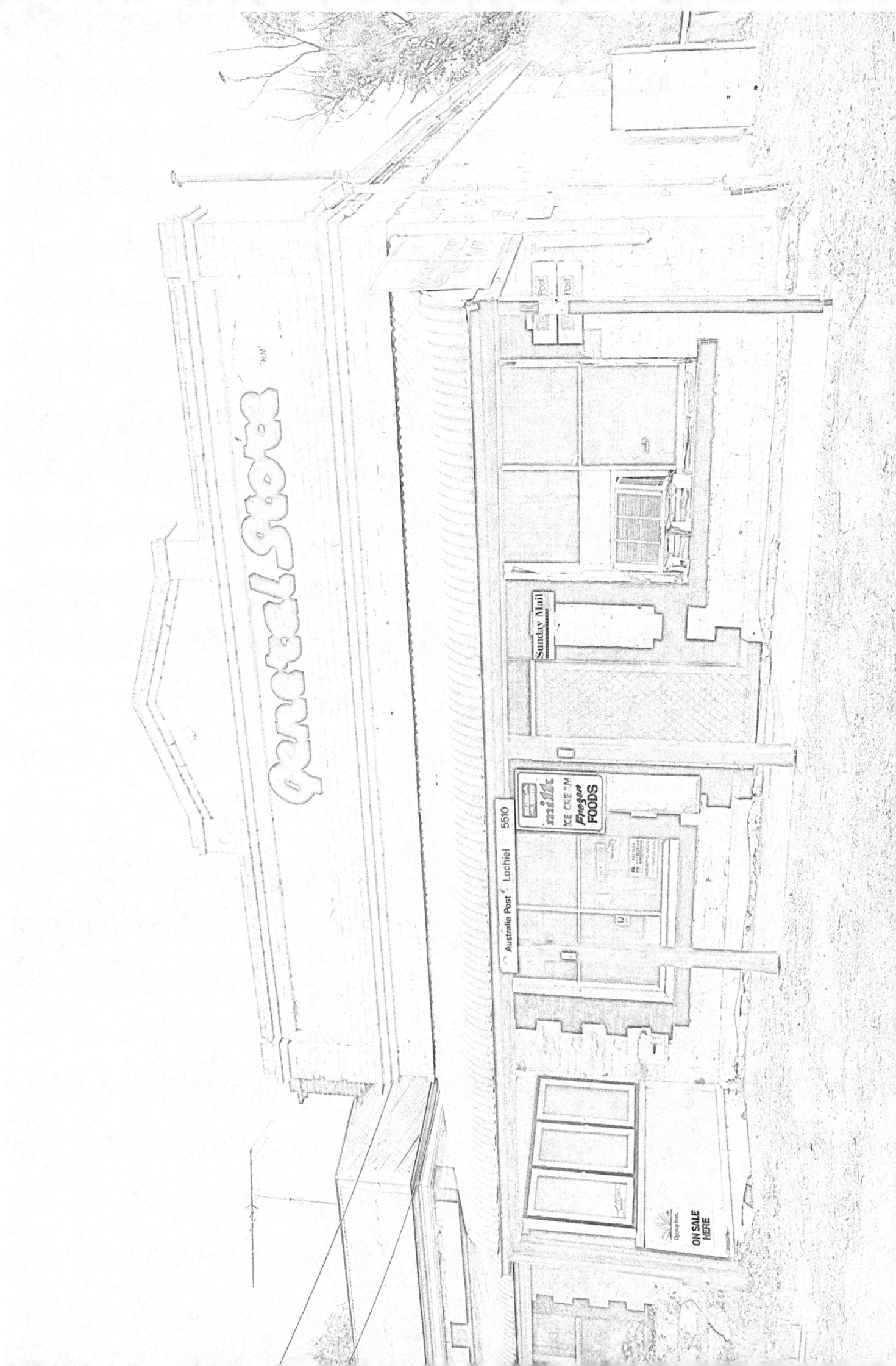

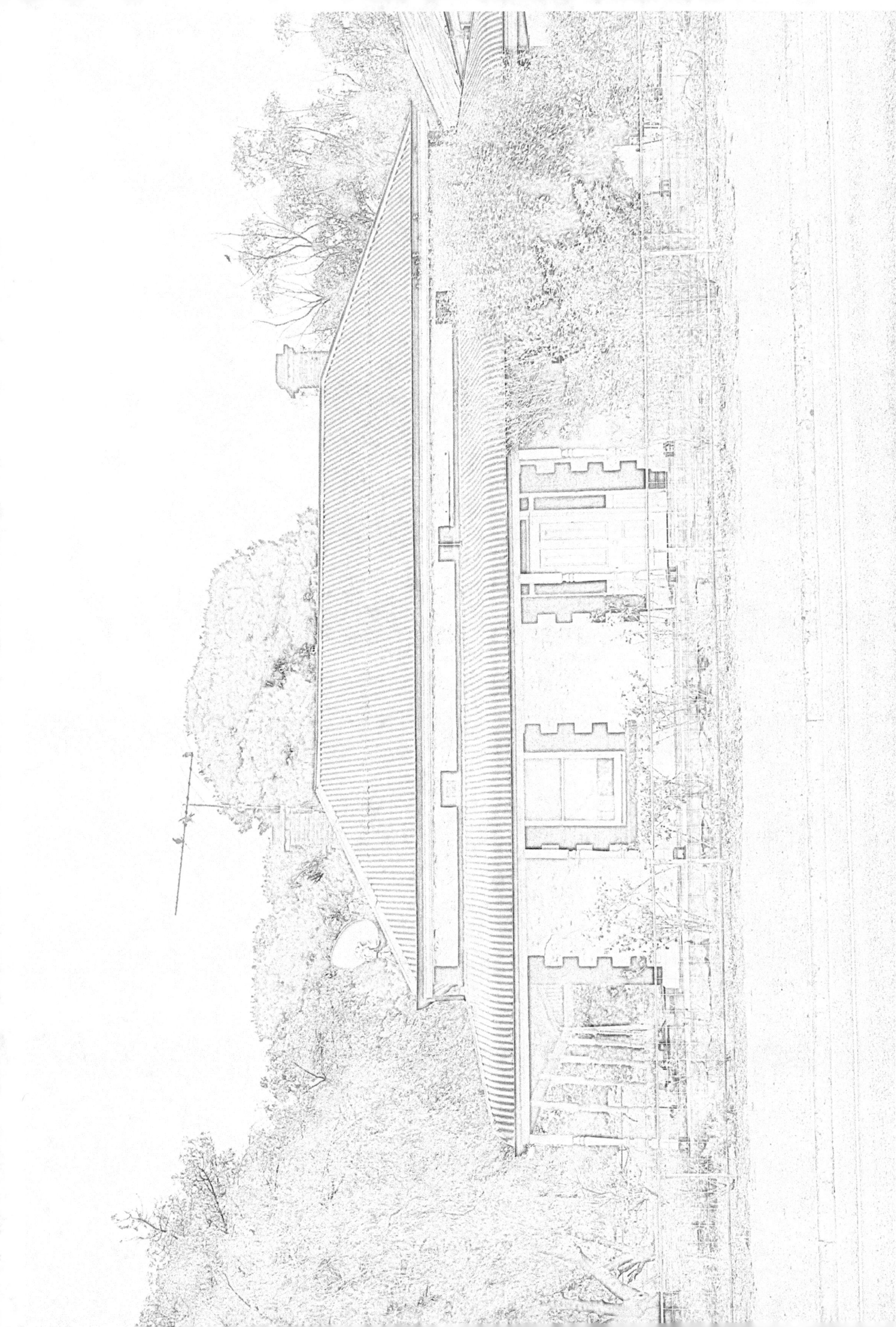

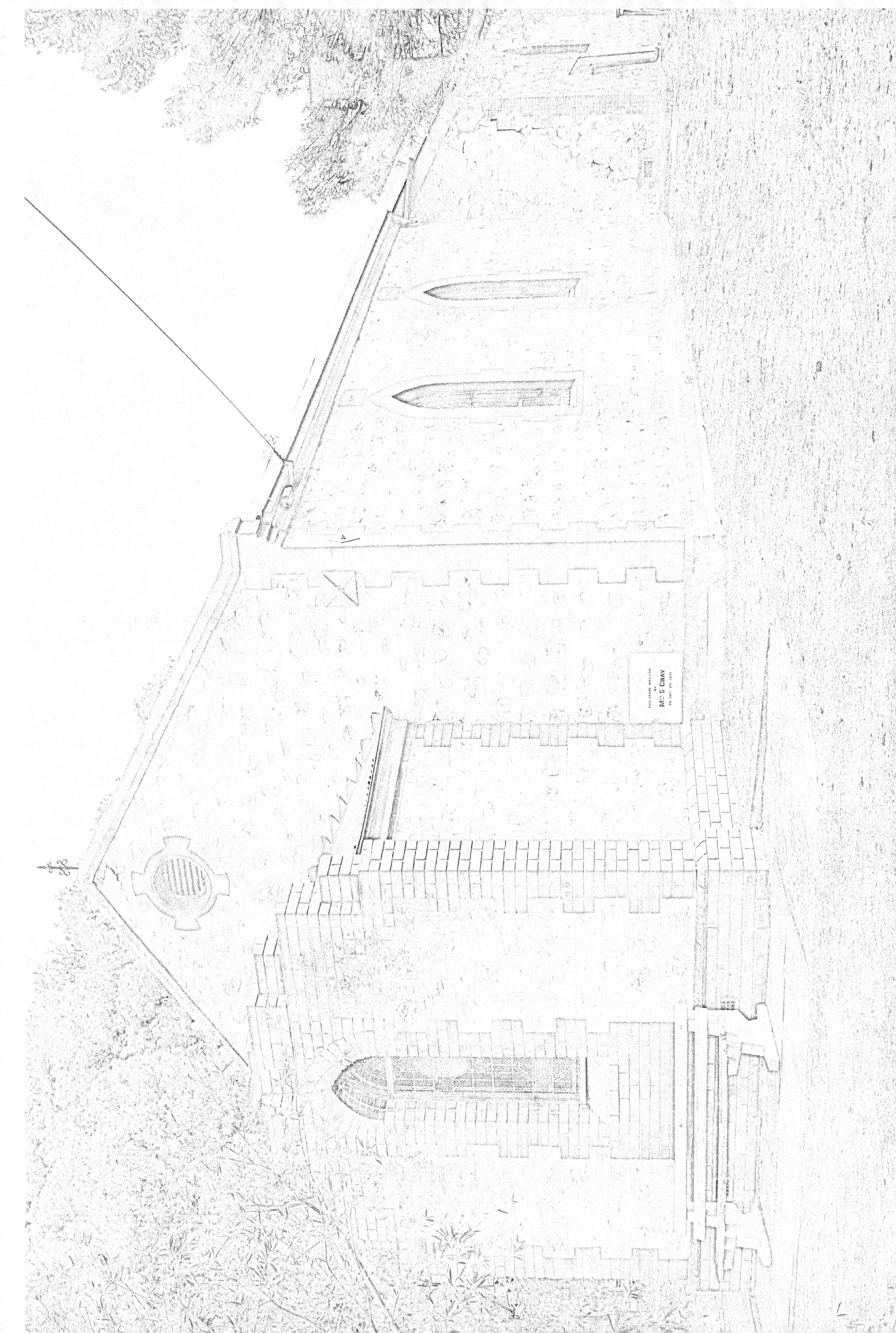

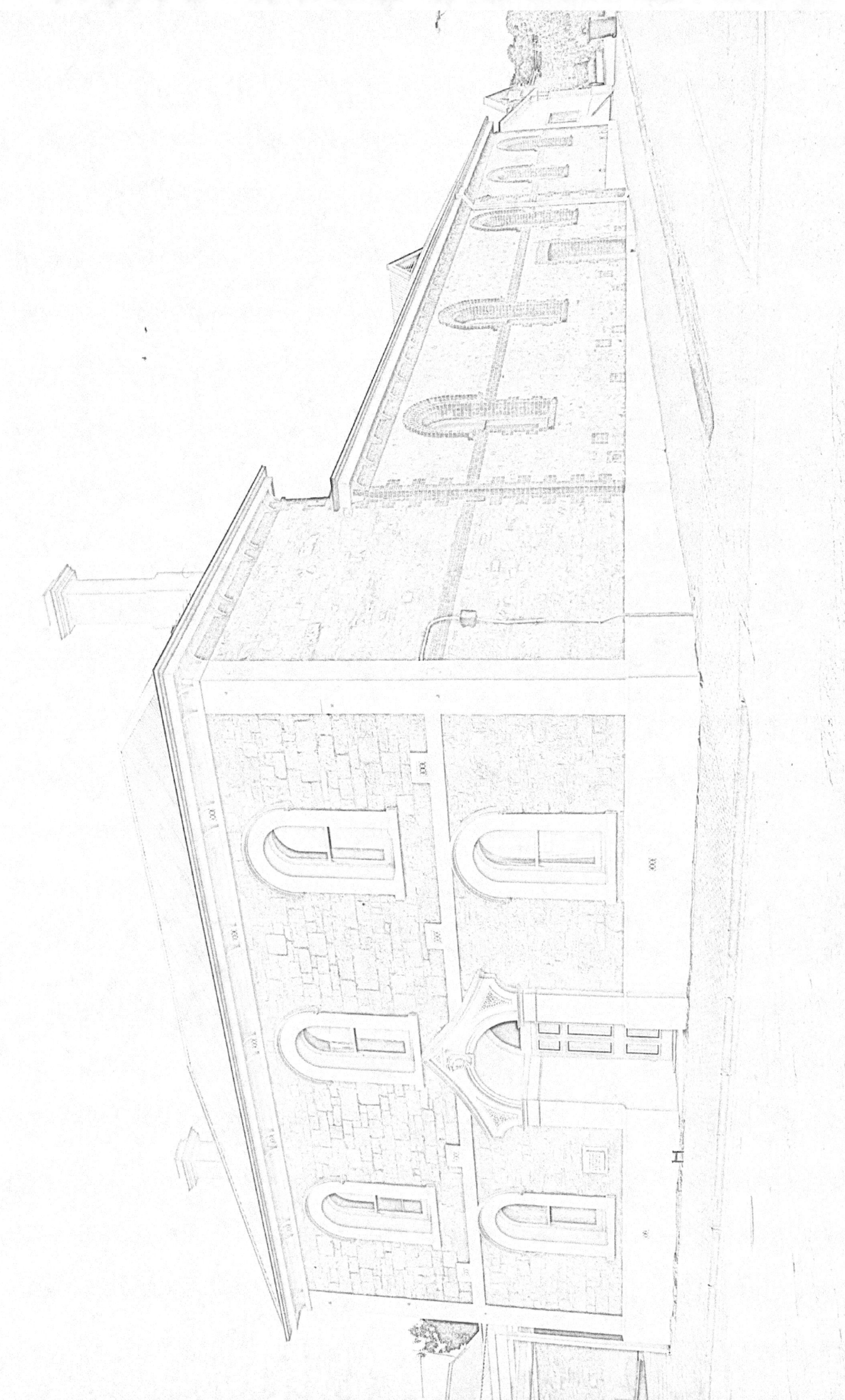

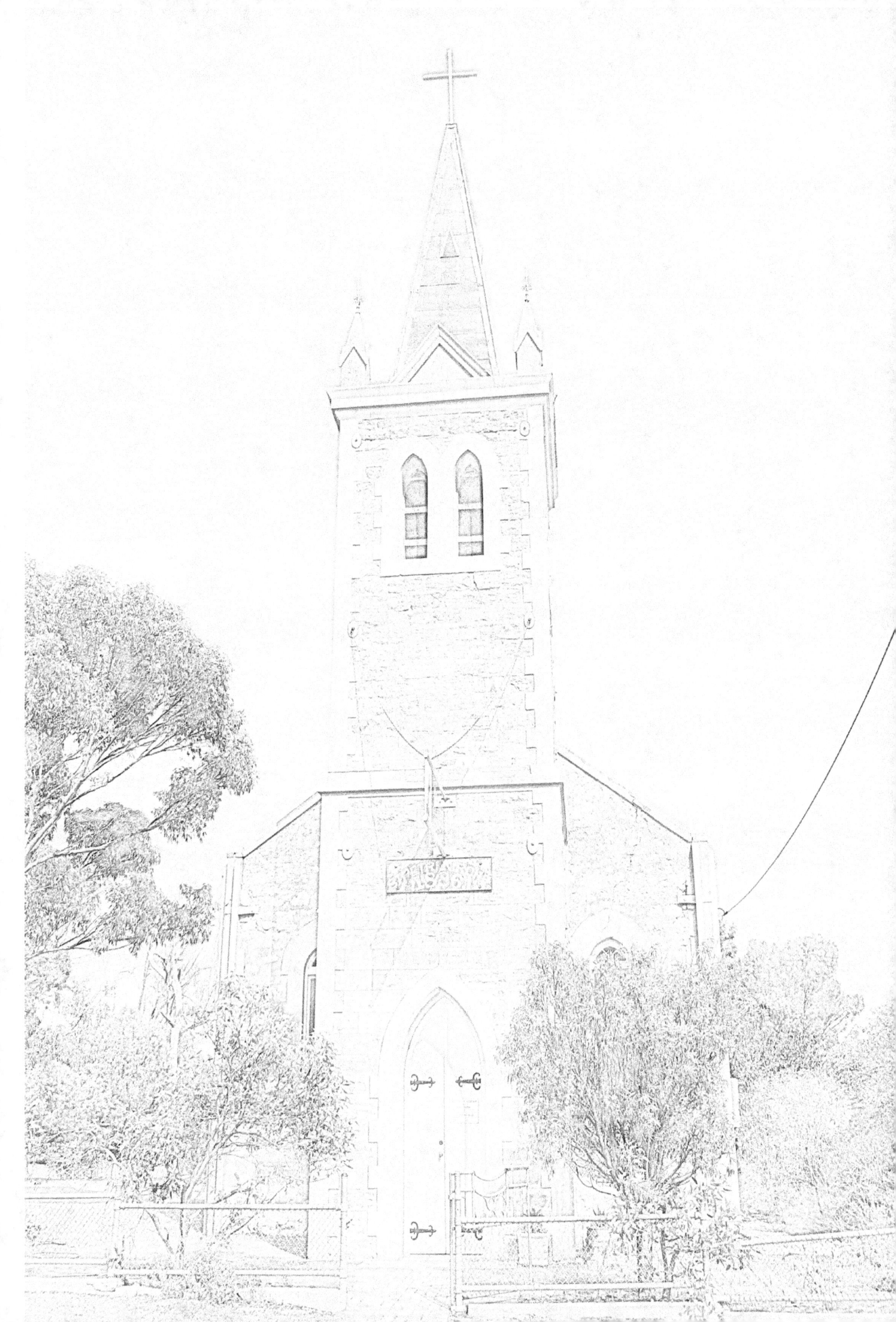

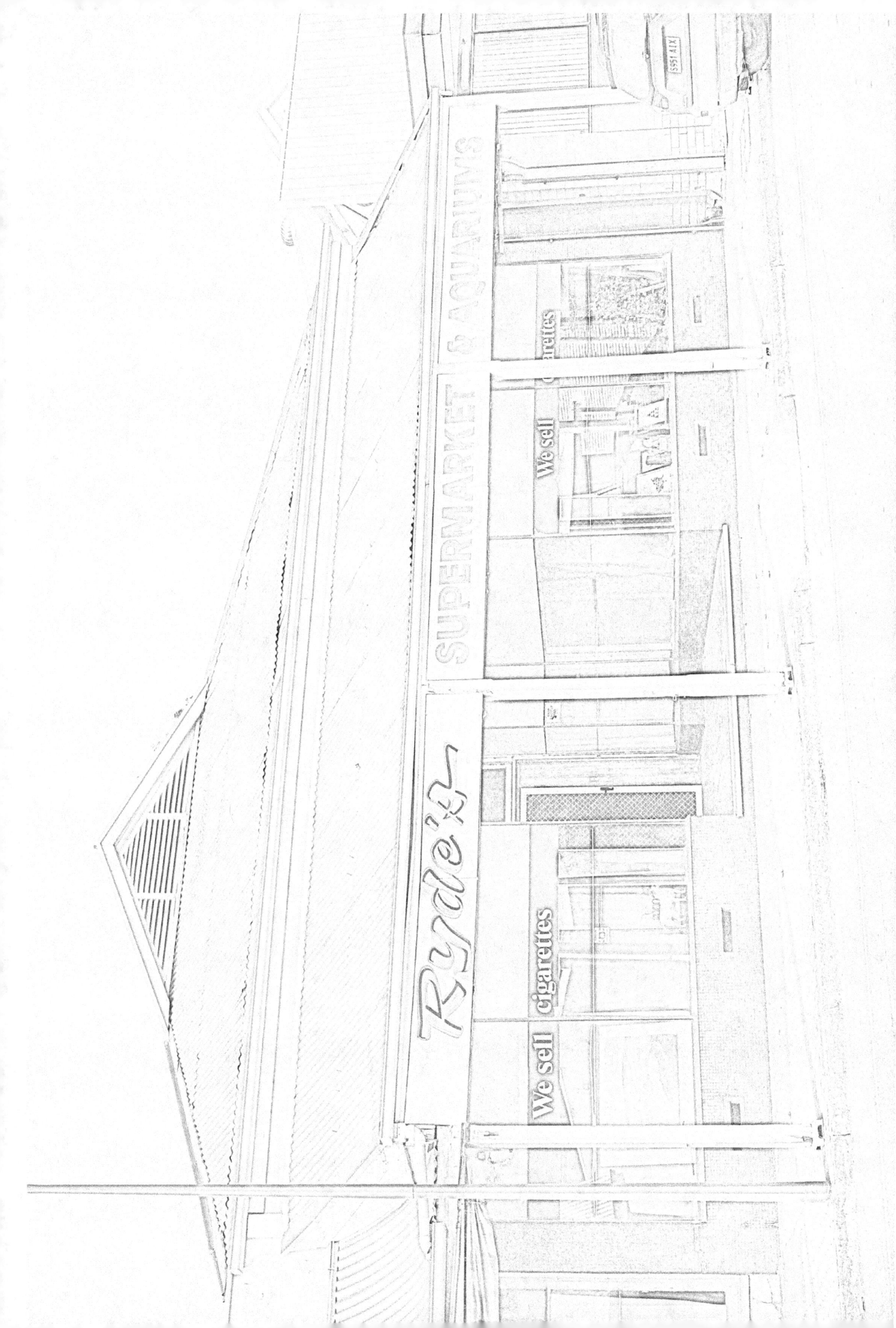

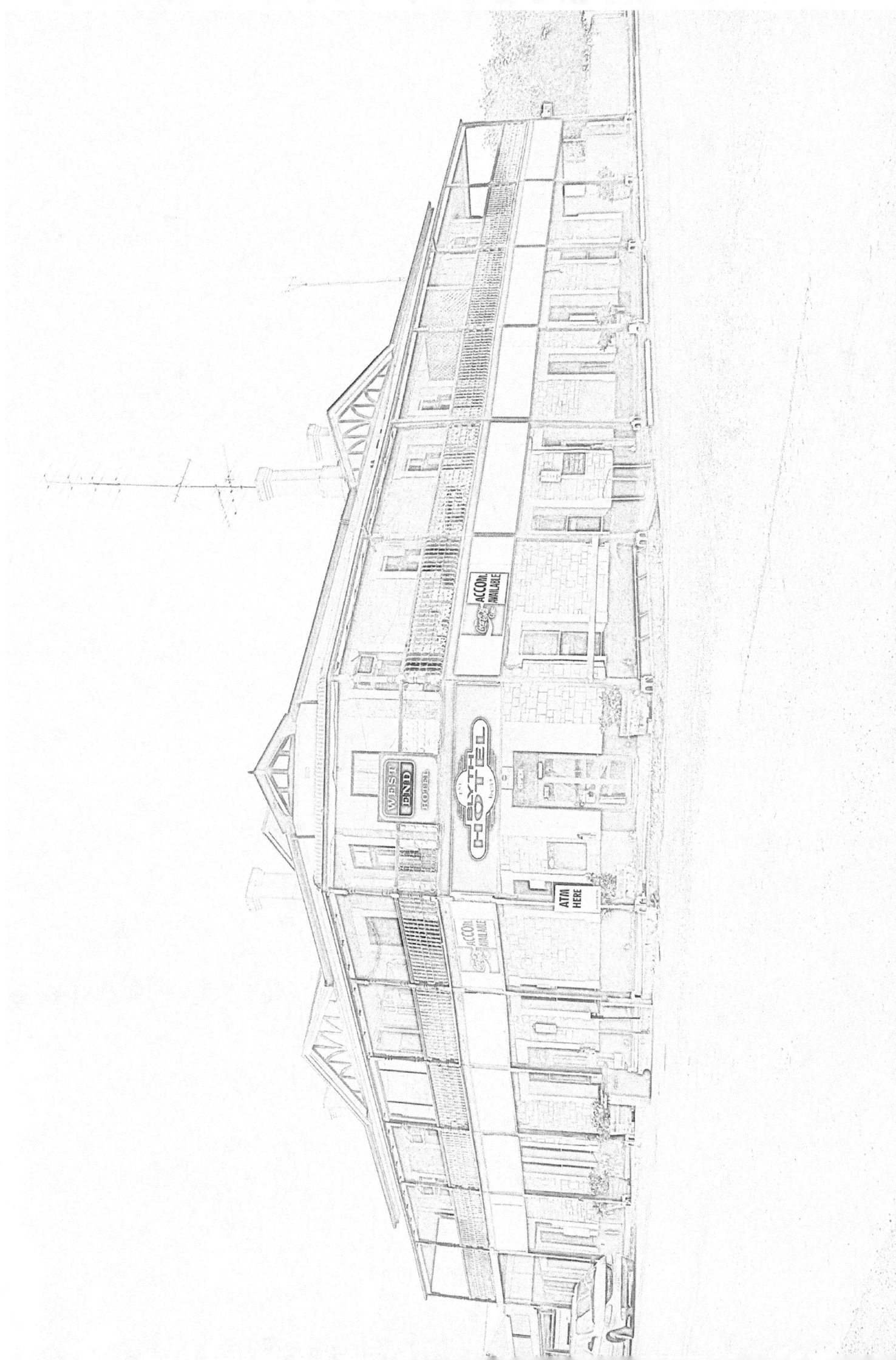

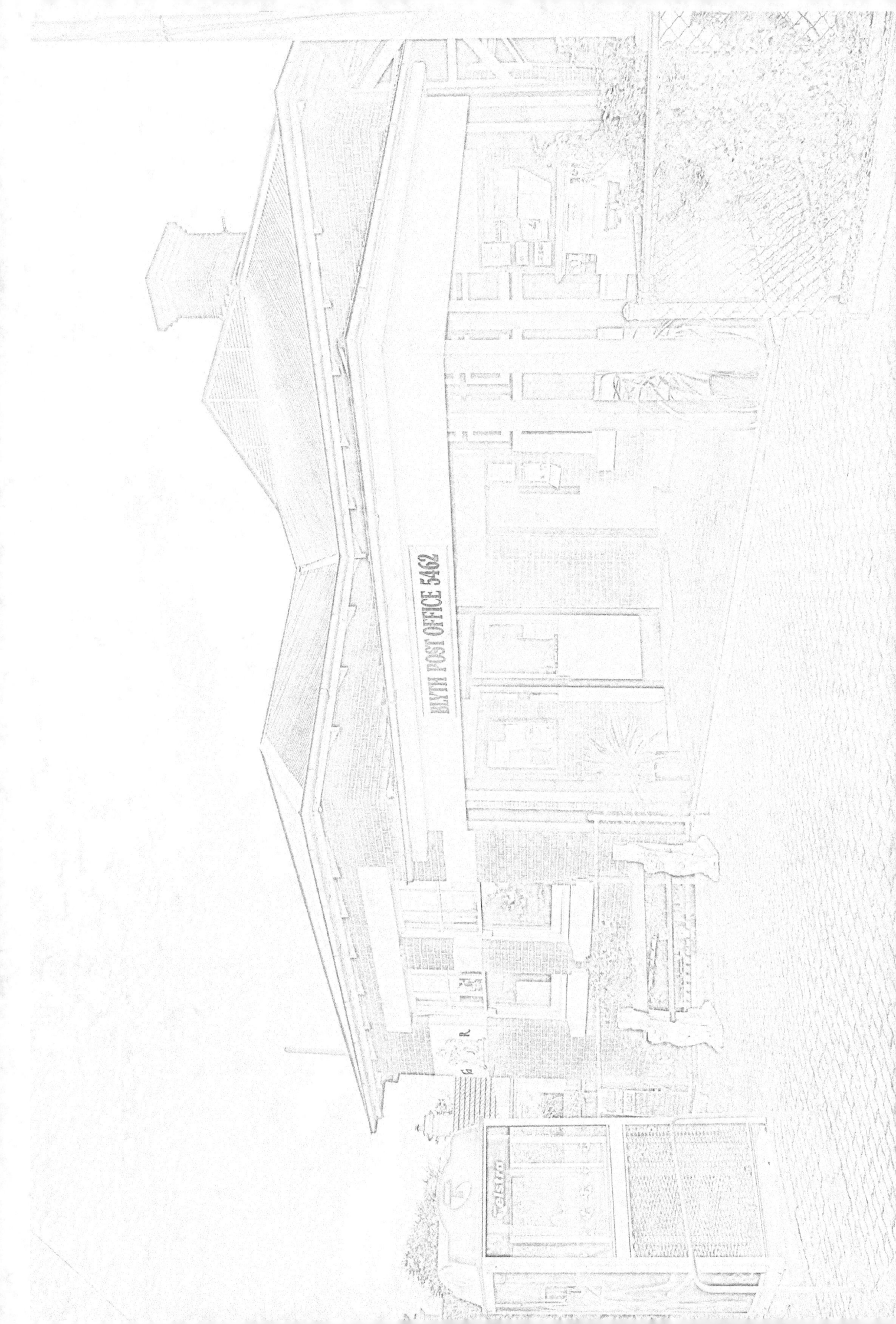

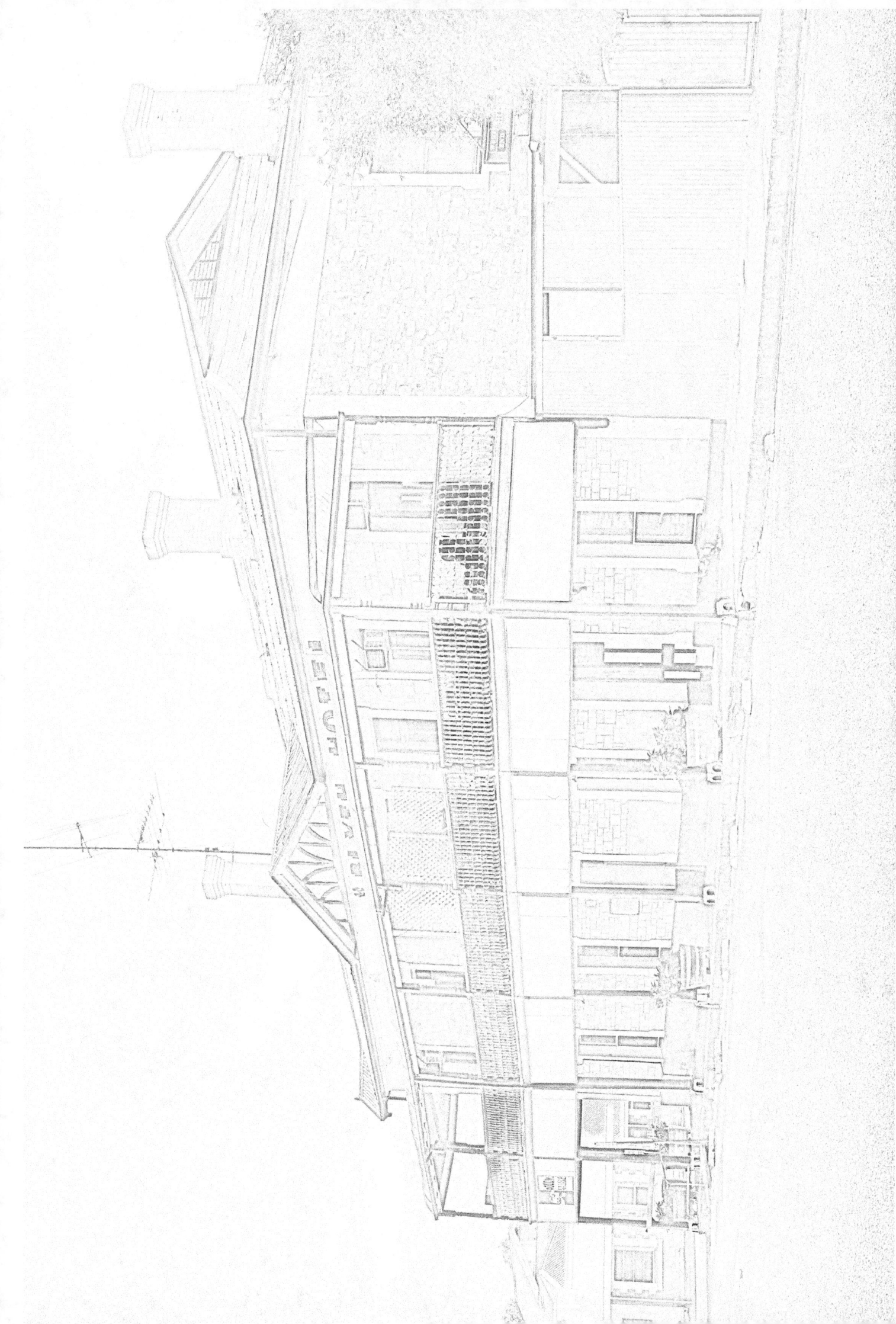

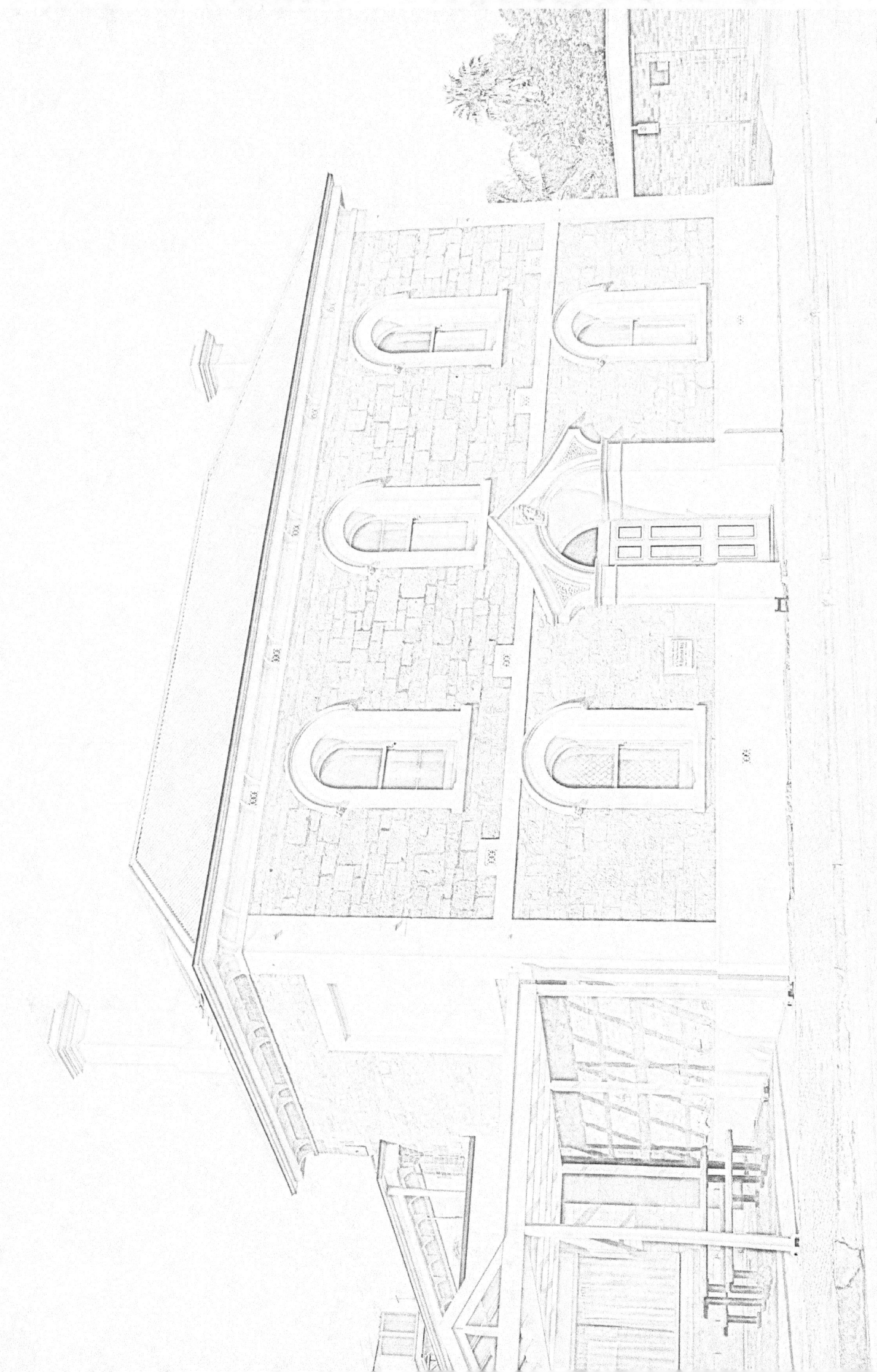

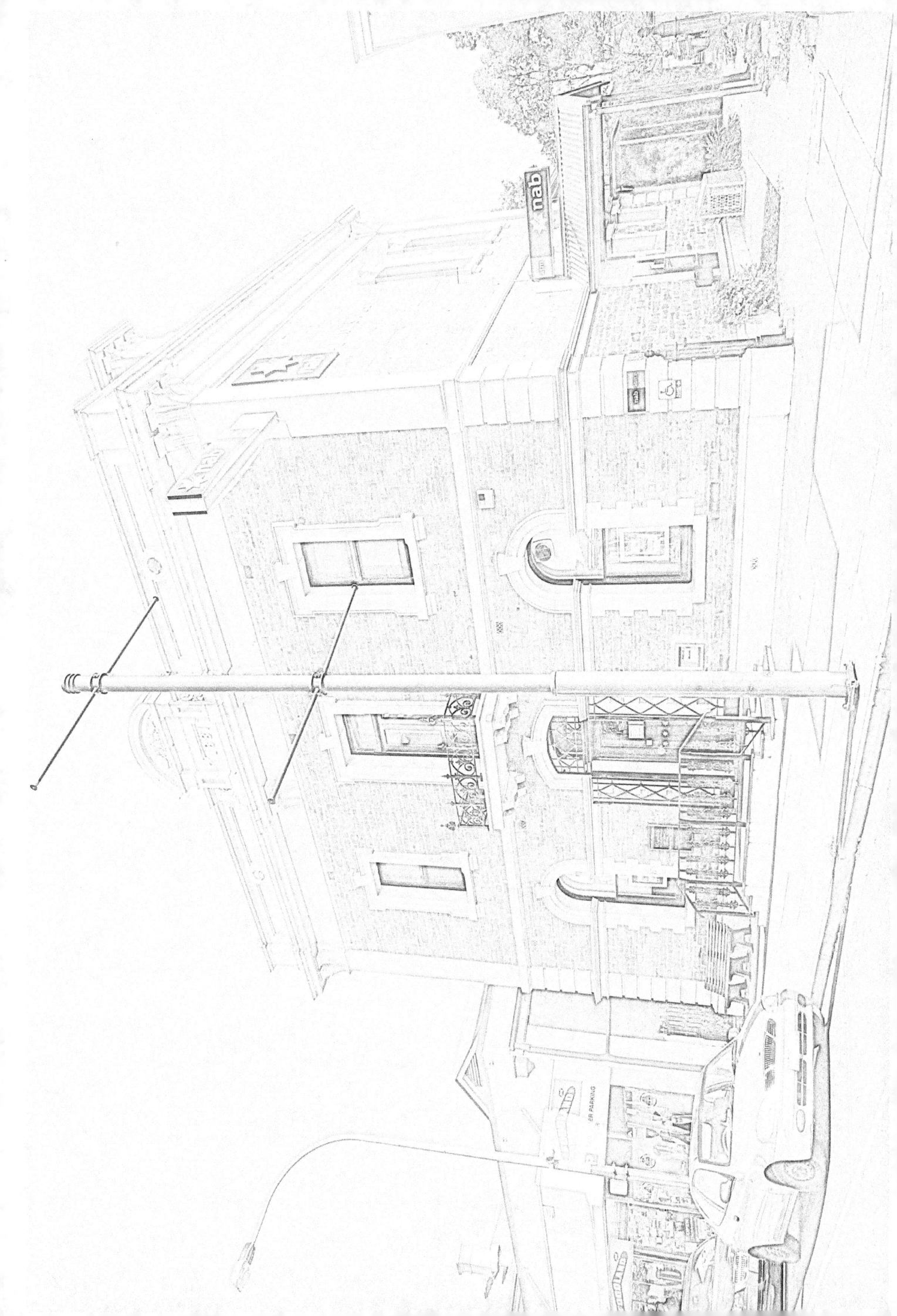

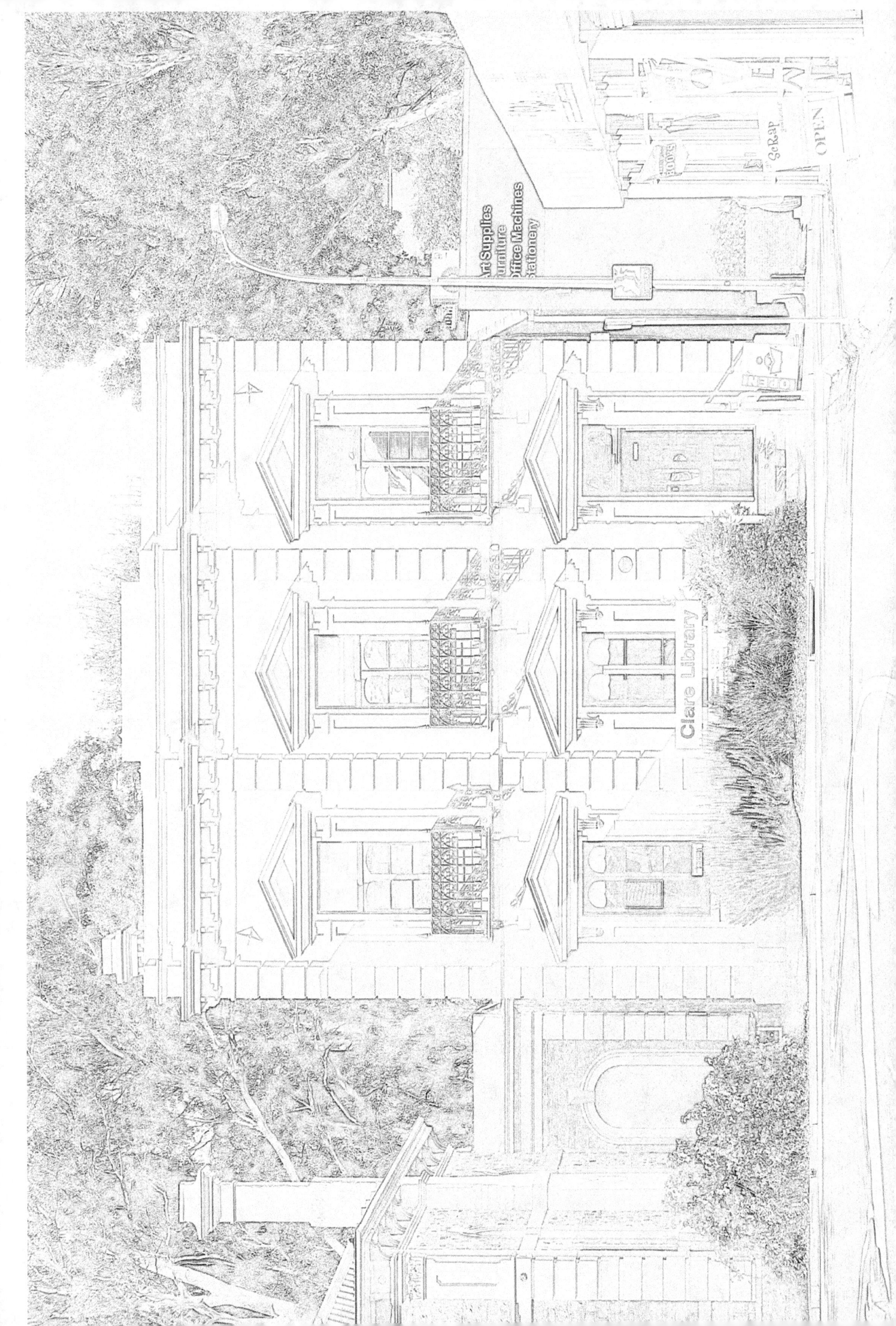

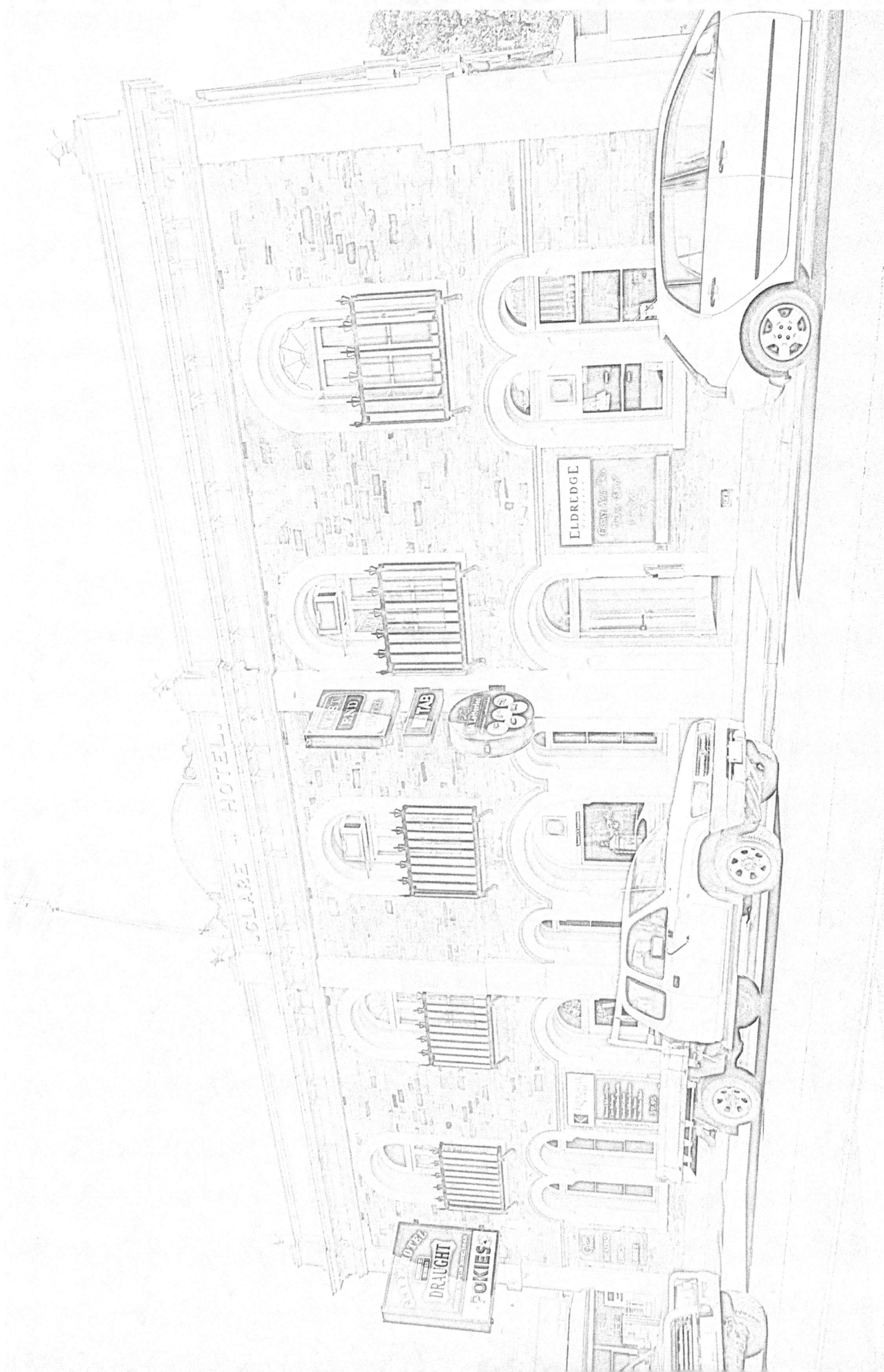